Heads Up, Taiwan

Bill Quinn

Taipei, Taiwan

First Printing, August, 2016

ISBN-13: 978-1539860754

ISBN-10: 1539860752

Teacher Bill Publishing
Minsheng East Road, Section 5, #48, 2-2
Taipei, Taiwan, R.O.C. 105

www.teacherbill.com

Acknowledgments

The writer of any book is just one person in the process. Along the way many people help—without them books don't get done. I'm grateful to have so many people help along the way.

Thank you to Doris Brougham 彭蒙惠 and Simon Hung 洪善群 for your support, and for believing in me and this book. Thanks to Amanda Jongepier and Fergus Fu 傅國雄 for your assistance. I also had editorial input from Steve Marth, Bryan Hagerla, Daniel Bastke and Bruce Bolen. And I need to give a shout out to Daniel Bastke for providing the drawings—you perfectly drew what I had in mind.

Thank you Vicki Hsiao 蕭碧燕 for the Forward. Your help with this is bigger than you realize! My niece, Laura Quinn worked very hard on the cover—not easy. Also, thank you to Tony Chen 陳璽年 and Peggy Hsu 許燕青 for being my cover models, and Jessica Wu 吳芸寧 for taking the cover photos.

And I'd like to thank Josh Mooney, Henry Chen 陳彥衡, Andy Lu 盧雍凱, Yilia Yu 游欣嫻, Nini Chen 陳品妤, Trevor Chen 陳冠綸, Janet Lee 李嘉娜, Frank Chiou 邱百章, Claire Liu 劉硯菁 and Evelyn Wang 王盈萍 for letting me include you in the text.

None of us are an island—we need others to do good things.

A blessing in my life: Doris

Daniel Bastke

Table of Contents

Foreword

A life well lived is no accident. It takes planning, discipline, persistence, kindness, love, generosity and a sense of humor. Along the way things change, so we need to examine what we are doing on a regular basis, and make adjustments as needed.

Good financial management requires attention to details and flexibility. Good life management also requires attention to details and flexibility. Some things work for a period of time, then they need to be adjusted. The important thing is to evaluate and adjust, whether it's money, time, health or relationships. To not evaluate on a regular basis is irresponsible.

Bill Quinn raises some interesting issues in this book about our daily use of technology, and challenges us to evaluate what we do each day with our phones, the Internet and social media. This is important since we spend so much time with our devices. It's important to know if we are setting and reaching our goals in life, and if we are managing our most valuable asset, time.

And while we need to evaluate and manage our time for our own personal growth, Bill shows how this also affects our society. As a society, are we managing our time well and reaching our goals? These are important considerations during this time of unique challenges for Taiwan.

I've known Bill for ten years. During his time here in Taiwan he's been both a teacher and a student. He's done extensive training of students, business professionals and government officials, teaching not just English, but life skills and professional development to thousands of people. And he's been a student—a student of Taiwan, studying our culture, the business environment, the education system and social landscape.

A good teacher asks questions that force students to think. I hope you take time to think about the issues raised in this book.

Vicki Hsiao 蕭碧燕

(A special note from Bill: Here is a link to Vicki's books—be sure to check them out!)

It's an honor to know Vicki :)

(Thanks to Christina Tsai 蔡佳倩 for recording the Foreword audio.)

Introduction

"The unexamined life is not worth living."

Socrates

How can you create a brighter future for yourself, and help make Taiwan better?

Throughout this book I often mention the term "critical thinking". Critical thinking is;

- Looking beyond the obvious
- Asking questions about what is known, searching for the unknown
- Analyzing and evaluating the information gathered from those questions
- Using that analysis/evaluation process to make more informed choices
- Applying those choices to improve our behaviors, beliefs and actions

It's important to apply critical thinking to many things in life—our work, careers, education, relationships, marriage, activities, health and money. While we don't want to "over-think", we do need to evaluate things occasionally to see if they help us to achieve our purpose in life.

In this book I highlight the importance of critical thinking as it applies to our use of smartphones, tablets, the Internet, social media and games. Over the past ten years our society has been transformed as devices have become part of our hand, and looking at those devices a huge part of our being.

That's the "What" of our behavior. How this behavior affects Taiwan society has fascinated me, as I've seen massive shifts in how we interact and don't interact with others. Yes, the entire world has changed with this digital revolution, but Taiwan has its own unique issues which I've observed.

Our devices can be awesome tools for communicating, getting work done and finding information. But for many of us our devices, the Internet, social media and games have overtaken our lives, far beyond mere communications, work and information.

Most of us have never really examined the "Why" of our behavior—why do my devices and their platforms dominate so much of my time? And most of us have not thought about the consequences of our behavior—what impact does this have on my life, on my relationships, on my purpose in life and on Taiwan society as a whole?

It would be silly to suggest that we give up on our phones, tablets, social media, the Internet and games—they're amazing technologies with great benefits. But, it would also be silly to not do some critical thinking about something that dominates our lives on a daily basis.

Are you (and Taiwan) getting better, staying the same, or getting worse?

If better, then how so?

If we stay the same, is maintaining the status quo a good long-term plan?

If worse, then how do you change this?

This book includes many pictures of what I see every day, at an increasing rate. It might seem harsh for me to shine such a spotlight on our behavior, but sometimes we need a dose of reality. I'm sure you'll recognize many of the situations.

I've also included many links, via QR codes, to the articles and videos that I cite as reference. Including QR codes that allow digital access via phones and tablets may seem a bit contradictory to my message, but to reach my audience I need to go where they are—on their devices. The reference articles and videos provide more information to the points I discuss, so I suggest that you download an app (they're free) that reads QR codes. That way you can access these valuable sources of further information.

If you want to listen to the audio of this book, go to my website, www.teacherbill.com, or visit my Facebook page for links to the readings.

I love Taiwan. But you don't need another foreigner telling you how great the food is, how lovely the scenery is, and how nice the people are—you already know all of that. I see a future full of big challenges for Taiwan. We're not going to meet those challenges with so many of us not engaging each other, focusing only on our phones. Taiwan's future depends on us.

Are we individually making ourselves better, and thus Taiwan better?

Is your head up, ready to meet the oncoming challenges?

Do we ask the right questions?

Links for audio

 www.teacherbill.com

 Bill's Facebook page

If you have problems getting the audio download, send me an email at quinnbill@gmail.com

Key Words and Terms

Over-think (v)—to think too much

Evaluate (v)—to analyze if something is good or bad

Highlight (v)—to focus on certain things

Transform (v)—to change from one way of being to another way of being

Massive (adj)—very large, huge

Interact (v)—talking or doing things with other people

Awesome (adj)—great, super

Overtake (v)—to control, to defeat

Dominate (v)—to control in all ways

Consequences (n)—results, outcomes

Impact (n)—effect

Maintaining the status quo (figure of speech)—keeping things the same

Reality (n)—the way things are

Cite (v)—to identify a source of information

Contradictory (adj)—two things that seem opposite to each other

Engage (v)—to give attention to others, exchange words, thoughts and ideas

1

Bridges and islands

"Moderation in all things"

Why is everybody **obsessed** with their phones?

For 13 years I've taught English in Taiwan. My work is helping people to communicate. Not just learn English, but use the language, talk to others, give presentations, build confidence. Ten years ago my boss at ORTV, Doris Brougham, gave me a copy of Rick Warren's *The Purpose Driven Life*, and one of the exercises in the book is to write down your purpose, or we might call it a "personal mission statement". Here's mine:

"To be a bridge between eastern and western cultures."

When I thought about how to **accomplish** that, I **distilled** my purpose down to a single word:

"Smile"

A smile can be the beginning of something great. It opens the door of interacting.

Teaching English is simply a **vehicle** for living my purpose, but it's more than just teaching a language; my passion is to encourage people to communicate, to engage with others—not just pass tests. And while I've enjoyed teaching English here in Taiwan and have met thousands of wonderful students, the current state of affairs troubles me. I've seen a regression in interpersonal communications over the past 13 years, as the pandemic of head down behavior has accelerated on an exponential path. Today, as I make my way around Taipei, more and more people focus on their phones and tablets, disinterested in the people around them. We've become our own little islands.

It's hard to smile when heads are down, and it's challenging to build bridges when we create our own little islands.

Twelve, ten, eight years ago, people would talk to me. In the supermarket, at 7-11, or on the bus many people in Taipei would look at me, smile, and start conversations, either out of curiosity or to practice their English. That seldom happens anymore. It's rare if eye contact is made.

I hate to say this, but Taipei is not as friendly as it was when I first came here. In some ways it's become a cold place—instead of smiles, now there are blank expressions as people briefly glance up from their phones in order to avoid running into me. The people of Taiwan are nice and friendly—but you'd never know it with the increase of head-down behavior—which is kind of sad, since the people here are often rated in polls as some of the nicest people on Earth.

It's not that I expect people to speak English with me; it's not necessary—they can speak Mandarin, and I'll give it a try with my so-so Mandarin. (Even when I speak Mandarin it doesn't always compute with people—they see my face and subconsciously decide they don't understand me.) What I've also noticed is that local people hardly even speak Mandarin or Taiwanese to each other. Instead, we isolate in our digital world, not being present in the moment, unavailable to others, unaware of our surroundings, closed off to serendipity.

Does it matter?

Taipei, like most big cities, is a sea of strangers. Millions of people moving about, racing to their destinations, herding into MRT cars and buses, clogging busy sidewalks and marketplaces, racing on scooters between red lights. The people of Taiwan that I came to know and love are lively, engaging, cheerful and pleasant. But we're gradually losing those qualities as we turn silent to strangers, glancing up from our phones only to navigate our way past bodies we don't take time to acknowledge as other humans just like us.

There's a great distance between us, even though we are inches apart. Our handheld distractions leave no time or mental space for even minimal verbal communications.

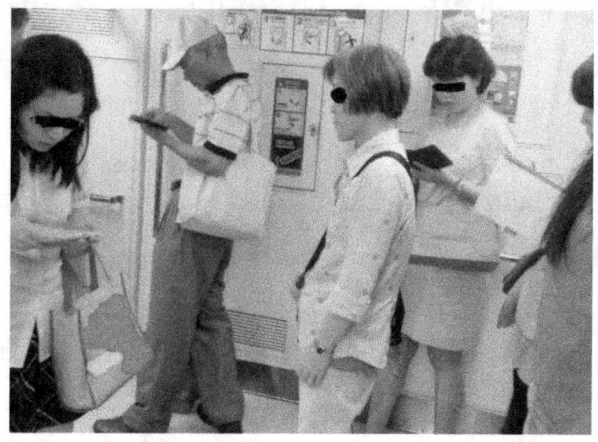

While this societal shift has been joked about and dramatized, we've never really asked why we engage in so much digital behavior, or weighed the cost on our individual development and the collective culture. There are disturbing consequences, personally and societally, that evade our consciousness as we drift deeper into our digital malaise.

Certainly, technology has benefits—I'm not advocating destruction or avoidance of our gadgets and social media—

smartphones and tablets are great tools. What I am advocating is "Moderation in all things". Which leads to this question:

Do you control your devices, or do they control you?

Because the answer to that question is what matters.

Instead of just shrugging our shoulders and saying "That's just the way it is" or "What can you do?" we need to ask the right questions, not just accept the status quo. Questioning the status quo is the beginning of critical thinking. "Does this help me to get better?" is a good place to start with any activity that we spend significant time on. And we spend a lot of time on our devices.

I've asked many people here "Why is everybody obsessed with their phones?" and the two most common replies are;

"We're bored"

"We're lonely"

Let's deal with "We're bored" first (I'll address "We're lonely" later).

"We're bored" leads to the next question: Why are we bored?

I think it's because few of us have ever clearly defined our life goals and life purpose.

Which leads to the next question: Why no life goals or life purpose?

Because nobody showed us how to set goals or define our life purpose.

Our parents didn't; our teachers didn't; our friends didn't. Setting goals and defining life purpose are very specific things that require us to think about what it is we wish to accomplish in life and how we wish to serve the world around us. Unfortunately, most people never sit down and write these out. Instead, most of us drift through life, waiting for someone else to tell us what to do. We've never written down our goals and purpose, so then we fill in the gaps with distractions from our boredom.

16

This starts when we're young: our parents send us to school, we study, and we have tests. We start well, being told what to do. But later, without specific guidance and left to our own devices, we drift. This continues into adulthood for most people. Life becomes a series of dreams—"I wish I had more money, a bigger house, a better job, I hope to win the lottery." Usually just dreams that we hope come true, without any written plan.

Life's a screen

I want you to set goals and accomplish them, to define your purpose in life, and make this world a better place. But you're not going to do this staring at your phone or tablet all day.

In the past two years, on two occasions I didn't use my smartphone for thirty days, and I also stopped using social media (mainly Facebook) twice for thirty days. The results were illuminating—I discovered that I didn't need my phone or Facebook as much as I thought I did.

I highly recommend that you try this digital diet. Go on a smartphone fast and/or a social media fast for thirty days. Yes, it seems extreme, but what you'll discover is;

1. **You will survive**.
2. Very few people will notice that you're not connected. **Most people won't miss you**. I'm sorry—it's revealing.
3. The people that really matter will still be in your life, just in different ways. You will quickly learn who really cares about you, who you care about and what really matters.
4. Your free time expands and **you'll get more sleep**. More sleep = more energy = more goals accomplished.
5. You'll notice things and people you hadn't noticed before.
6. You will have time to think, to contemplate matters, like your purpose in life.
7. This intellectual availability will free you up to set better goals, plan and execute great things.
8. Your critical thinking will improve, which leads to better daily decisions, which leads to better long-term decisions.

After 30 days you may return to your old digital habits, or you may find liberation in controlling your device, happily embracing the ancient wisdom of "Moderation in all things".

My job in this book is to get you to think about your personal digital habits, observe your surroundings, set goals, define life purpose and improve your time/life management. I think you'll like it, and I bet you'll be happier.

Key words and terms

Obsessed (adj)—too much attention, too much importance

Accomplish (v)—to complete a task, reach a goal

Distill (v)—get to the basic principle

Vehicle (n)—a tool used to accomplish something

Current state of affairs (figure of speech)—the way things are now

Regression (n)—to go backwards, the opposite of progress

Interpersonal (adj)—relations between two people

Pandemic (n)—a widespread disease

Accelerated (adj)—at a fast speed

Exponential (adj)—increasing at an increasing rate

Seldom (adj)—not often, rarely

Expression (n)—what our face looks like

Glance (v)—a quick look

Necessary (adj)—needed, important

Subconsciously (adv)—doing something without thinking

Unaware (adj)—not seeing, hearing or noticing things

Surroundings (n)—the area around us

Serendipity (n)—when something good happens that was unexpected

Destination (n)—a place that we are going to

Clog (v)—to prevent passage or movement through something

Navigate (v)—to make changes in a journey as needed

Acknowledge (v)—to show that you see and recognize things/people

Shift (n/v)—movement

Collective (adj/n)—everybody in society

Disturbing (adj)—upsetting, something that causes worry

Evade (v)—to avoid something, or not be aware of it

Consciousness (n)—awareness, thinking about something

Malaise (n)—a lack of energy, lack of interest

Advocate (v)—to promote something you believe in

Moderation (n)—balance, enough, not too much of something

Shrug (v)—to move your shoulders up and down

Address (v)—to deal with something

Unfortunately (adv)—not good, not lucky, disappointing

Drift (v)—to move about in no particular direction

Distraction (n)—something that takes our attention away

Guidance (n)—advice, counsel

Left to our own devices (figure of speech)—doing things on our own without any instruction

Illuminating (adj)—educational, new ideas or ways of thinking

Fast (n)—doing without something for a period of time

Contemplate (v)—to think deeply about something

Execute (v)—to put a plan into action

Liberation (n)—freedom from something

Embrace (n)—fully accepting something

2

The Dalai Lama does not own a smartphone

"The mass of men lead lives of quiet desperation, and go to the grave with the song still in them."

Henry David Thoreau

What are you looking for?

There's a gap in time—you reflexively look at the phone, scroll Facebook or LINE:

What are you looking for?

I've asked groups of students this question, and the resounding answer is . . .

"I don't know"

Millions of people fill their days looking for "I don't know". Mostly, we're just looking for something, anything to fill the gaps—those moments and minutes in the day that add up to a significant chunk of life. We seek distraction because we don't know what to do with the gaps. We're uncomfortable with gaps, we're uncomfortable with silence.

Now, our default mechanism is to look at our phone or tablet the moment there's a visual or audio gap, looking for anything to give some meaning to our life, or just kill some time. (Killing time is okay, in moderation, but not when it becomes habitual.)

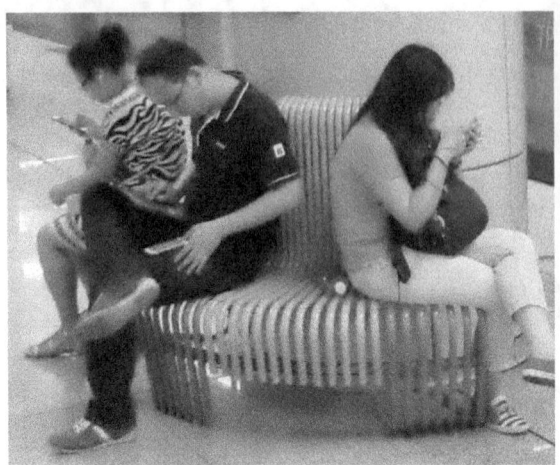

Phone challenge: The next time you meet silence or inactivity and are tempted to grab your phone, try to resist the urge. Spend a few minutes in silence, not looking at a screen—we look at screens all day. Give your eyes a rest and your mind a chance to be in the moment.

If we don't know what we're looking for, the digital collective defines what is important. Days, weeks and months string together in a ceaseless stream of posts, photographs, LINE messages, FB comments and likes. Today's stream looks just like yesterday's, and serves as a prelude to tomorrow's stream. It's SOS (Same Old Stuff), leading us to the same place; a state of emptiness, which we try to fill with more scrolling, only to be trapped in a vortex of the mundane. We're consuming mass quantities of "digital junk food".

Daily we're inundated with the irrelevant, drowning in a deluge of unimportant information, but we never consider the causes or, more importantly, the consequences of our addiction to distraction. It's not just social media that drains our intellectual and emotional batteries; phones and tablets have made the Internet constantly available, filling our minds with information, much of it trivial, incomplete and often inaccurate. In one of his sermons, Pastor Rick Warren mentioned the popular game Trivial Pursuit, and how our lives have become a trivial pursuit. We spend our time and energy consuming mass quantities of information, most of which will be forgotten by tomorrow.

Personally, I was living trivial pursuit, spending way too much time looking at stories, news, sports, videos, etc. on the Internet. I'm not sure it made me any smarter; rather, it just confused me and delayed meaningful goal work. Almost everything on the Internet is designed to generate clicks, which drives advertising revenues for content providers. As a result, I'm bombarded with headlines and stories aimed at provoking me. **It's not a recipe for finding peace and** contentment. I was spending hours and hours, each day, bouncing around the Internet and social media. My life was drifting off into the Google cloud.

Additionally, there are myriad games and videos to mesmerize us, lulling us into a semi-trance, not speaking, not hearing, and mostly looking through people as we glance up just in time to sidestep them on the sidewalk.

I read an article that contained this interesting statement;

"The Dalai Lama does not own a smartphone"

(link to the article)

He probably has more peace and contentment than me. If the Dalai Lama doesn't have a smart phone, why am I spending so much time on mine? (I'm sure his handlers have smartphones, but it's **instructive** to all of us that he isn't carrying one around, constantly checking it.)

<u>Are we better off?</u>

Over the past six or seven years smartphone and tablet use has **skyrocketed**.

Yes, we can execute more tasks and be connected constantly, and we have a **plethora** of information at our fingertips, but has the collective **psyche** of Taiwan improved, or gotten worse? Are we more joyful? Have our **stress** levels been reduced or risen? Have we discovered our purpose? Is your life better? Have we found our **bliss**, or do we just **chase our tails**?

Looking at the phone has become the "distraction reflex"— have you ever noticed how we instantly look at the screen when a moment presents itself, rather than living in the moment? Here's an article that talks about living in the moment, and practicing mindfulness, rather than giving in to reflex distraction;

We're letting the moments, days, weeks and months of our lives be consumed without even realizing it, caught up in an illusion of urgency, lured by beeps, bells and notifications.

Why do we need constant distraction?

At the beginning of this chapter is a quote by Henry David Thoreau that addresses our existence;

"The mass of men lead lives of quiet desperation, and go to the grave with the song still in them."

So, how can we sing our song?

What we need to do is examine our activity—what we spend our time and energy on. In the next chapter I'll cover an easy exercise for you, which will help identify what your priorities should be. This will change how you interact with your phone and tablet.

Key Words

Reflexively (adv)—a physical reaction

Scroll (v)—to quickly roll through information, looking for something of interest

Resounding (adj)—very big, strong, a lot

Significant (adj)—a large amount, very important

Default (adj)—an automatic action

Mechanism (n)—a function, how something is done

Habitual (adj)—a habit that is done too much

Tempted (v)—the feeling of wanting to do something

Resist (v)—choosing to not do something

Ceaseless (adj)—endless, constant, never ending

Prelude (n)—a preview of something in the future

Vortex (n)—a downward force that pulls things into it

Mundane (n/adj)—unimportant

Inundate (v)—to be flooded with something, overwhelmed

Irrelevant (adj)—not important to us

Drown (v)—to be covered by water, unable to breath

Deluge (n)—a lot of something, a heavy rain

Addiction (n)—something not good for us which we can't give up or quit doing

Drain (v)—to reduce, to lower something

Trivial (ajd)—facts and information that aren't important

Incomplete (adj)—missing something or several things

Inaccurate (adj)—wrong, not correct

Meaningful (adj)—having purpose, worth doing

Generate (v)—to create

Drive (v)—to create, to make something happen

Content (n)—material, text, information

Bombard (v)—to provide a large a very large amount of something

Provoke (v)—to cause anger or create a reaction

Contentment (n)—satisfied with the state of things

Myriad (n)—a very large number of something

Mesmerize (v)—to confuse, or cause a state of staring

Lull (v)—to create extreme relaxation

Trance (n)—not fully conscious, hypnotized

Sidestep (v)—to step to the side to avoid something

Instructive (adj)—educational, enlightening

Skyrocket (v)—to rise at a fast rate

Plethora (n)—many of something

Psyche (n)—a mental state, a way of feeling, thinking and being

Stress (n)—a feeling of pressure

Bliss (n)—happiness, satisfaction

Chase our tails (figure of speech)—to keep going around in circles, not making progress

Mindfulness (n)—thinking carefully about things and situations

Illusion (n)—something that appears to be real, but isn't

Urgency (n)—a sense of doing things now

Lure (v)—to be attracted to something

Notification (n)—something that lets you know something has happened or will happen

Existence (n)—the state of being, living

Desperation (n)—a feeling of emptiness, hopelessness

Priorities (n)—important things that need to be done

3

Thinking Outside the Box, Operating in the Right Box

"What is important is seldom urgent and what is urgent is seldom important"

Dwight D. Eisenhower

The Eisenhower Matrix, applied by U.S. President Dwight D. Eisenhower, and made popular by Stephen Covey in his book *The 7 Habits of Highly Effective People*, lays out a matrix of things in our life—Urgent, Not Urgent, Important, Not Important. Here's what it looks like;

	Urgency	
High		Low
1. Urgent and Important (Do it now)	2. Not Urgent and Important (Plan)
3. Urgent and Not Important (Avoid if possible)	4. Not Urgent and Not Important (Low priority)

Importance — High / Low

For our long-term growth, box 2 is where we need to focus. But our devices and social media pull us into box 3, with our daily existence being filled with "urgent" things that aren't really important. The problem is that the more time we spend in box 3, the less time we spend in box 2, thus aborting the planning and work that go into creating the life we hope for. Box 2 is our goals and life purpose box.

What's also a problem is that many of us spend too much time in box 4 each day, which often is wasted time. Box 4 is okay when you need to relax, but our phones and tablets have magnified its impact on our daily lives.

Here's a breakdown of each box—which box do you live in?

Box 1—Urgent and Important: work responsibilities, daily family responsibilities, your boss.

Box 2—Important but Not Urgent: long-term business plans, strategic thinking, goals, life purpose planning, investment planning.

Box 3—Urgent and Not Important: gossiping on LINE, scrolling on Facebook for the latest updates, hot celebrity news, whatever the news media wants you to look at, complaining about the boss/company policy, waiting 30 minutes in line at Starbucks because it's 2-for-1 Day.

Box 4—Not Important and Not Urgent: Playing Candy Crush, watching Korean soap operas, watching sports (a big time waster for most Americans), spending Friday and Saturday night at the pub getting drunk, long hours of KTV.

In the diagram on the next page, I have filled in my boxes as an example;

	Urgency	
High		Low

1. Urgent and Important (Do it now)	2. Not Urgent and Important (Plan)
A. Teach class at 9 am B. Meet with my boss at 11 am C. Deliver package to client	A. Work on website design B. Write some text for my next book C. Plan marketing strategy
3. Urgent and Not Important (Avoid if possible)	4. Not Urgent and Not Important (Low priority)
A. Stand in line 1 hour for today's doughnut sale B. Exchange many texts about today's NBA game C. Discuss latest office rumor	A. Watch a football game for 3 hours B. Watch many cat videos on YouTube C. Play a video game for 1 hour

(Importance — vertical axis, High to Low)

Bill's matrix

Now, in the diagram below, you fill in the boxes of your life;

	Urgency	
High		Low

1. Urgent and Important (Do it now)	2. Not Urgent and Important (Plan)
A. B. C.	A. B. C.
3. Urgent and Not Important (Avoid if possible)	4. Not Urgent and Not Important (Low priority)
A. B. C.	A. B. C.

(Importance — vertical axis, High to Low)

Your matrix

We have to do the things in box 1. What we need to do is some critical thinking about boxes 3 and 4, and shift the time and energy from those boxes to box 2.

It's easy to get stuck in box 3. Urgency is alluring, but it only gives us the illusion of being busy—we're busy with the wrong things, spending hours on meaningless motion. Successful people spend little time in box 3. They either ignore the items that arise there, or delegate the ones that must be dealt with (which are few).

Successful people do spend some time in box 4, but that time is limited, and usually specifically targeted, such as vacations or scheduled relaxation periods. How successful people handle boxes 3 and 4 is called good time management, which requires discipline and good decision making. (Unfortunately, most of us are just busy looking busy.)

How do we get better at managing our boxes?

It's all about goal setting, which we'll cover in the next chapter.

<u>Key Words</u>

Matrix (n)—an arrangement of rows and columns

Abort (v)—to end something, stop a process

Magnify (v)—to make something larger than it really is

Breakdown (n/v)—an explanation of things

Strategic (adj)—having a plan, thinking about the process

Gossip (v)—to talk about people and things, usually in an unproductive way

Alluring (adj)—very attractive

Meaningless (adj)—not important at all

Ignore (v)—to not give attention to something

Delegate (v)—to assign a task or work to someone else

Specifically (adv)—a particular item or plan

Targeted (v)—focused on one item

Discipline (n)—self-control

4

Aiming for the Stars, Landing on the Moon

"Begin with the end in mind"

Stephen Covey

"Who has written down their goals?"

At almost every seminar I give, whether it's at a school, university, company or government agency, I ask the audience that question.

If there are 20 people in the room, one person may raise their hand—that's 5% of the group—and this is true every time I ask this question. I can confidently say that only 5% of all the people in Taiwan have ever written down their goals (and this is probably true everywhere). I can also confidently say that a much larger percentage of highly successful people have written down their goals.

But goal setting isn't just about being "successful"—it's not just about making more money or getting promoted at work. Goal setting also helps to reduce our boredom, loneliness, depression and frustration. When we have our goals in writing we focus our time and energy on things that matter in life, so we're less likely to drift through days, weeks, months and years. If we don't set goals, somebody else will set them for us, or, the cyber-universe will tell you what's important, creating an ever-changing list of priorities that seldom leads to accomplishment.

Maybe they're reviewing their goal lists

Most of us dream about what we wish we had, but we're not doing much to make those dreams come true. We're not breaking out of the patterns that don't produce constructive results. Instead, we tend to complain, blame the system, or get comfortable in our misery, whether it's a job we don't like, a relationship that is unsatisfying or a bad habit that holds us back. Breaking out of these patterns requires work—thinking, planning, collaborating—and goal setting is the first step to changing our lives.

How to set goals

I've provided a goal worksheet in the next few pages that will get you started on changing your life, and managing your boxes better. Here are five key points to effective goal setting;

- You need short-term and long-term goals
- You need a time frame on each goal
- You need to be as specific as possible with each goal
- You need a reason as to why each goal is important to you
- You need to know what can be done on a daily basis to reach that goal

Here is the worksheet that I hand out at every seminar I give. You should take some time to carefully think about what goals you wish to set. I advise you to think big!

I am _____, and these are . . .

My goals for the next year:

1.

      This is important to me because:

      Today I must do this to reach this goal:

2.

      This is important to me because:

      Today I must do this to reach this goal:

3.

      This is important to me because:

      Today I must do this to reach this goal:

My goals for the next five years are:

1.

      This is important to me because:

      Today I must do this to reach this goal:

2.

> This is important to me because:
>
> Today I must do this to reach this goal:

3.

> This is important to me because:
>
> Today I must do this to reach this goal:

My goals for the next ten years are:

1.

> This is important to me because:
>
> Today I must do this to reach this goal:

2.

> This is important to me because:
>
> Today I must do this to reach this goal:

3.

> This is important to me because:
>
> Today I must do this to reach this goal:

You can write your goals in this book or do it on a separate piece of paper. At seminars I hand this worksheet out on a single piece of letter-sized paper, so you may want to do this on a separate piece of paper—it will give you more space to write. Then you can keep this sheet in a convenient place, because you will need to review it periodically.

At the minimum, you should review your goal sheet once a week in the first six months. This will keep you focused on your goals, and help you to adjust as necessary. You can rewrite your goal sheet over time, as you get older and things in your life change—but always keep your goal sheet handy, to remind you.

Be careful what you wish for

Here's something amazing about writing down your goals: most of your goals will be achieved! There's something magical about writing down your goals and setting a plan to make them happen. So write them down, be specific, and be bold! You may want to share your goal worksheet with someone close to you, someone you can trust. Doing that makes us more accountable to our goals, since we have shared them with another person. And that person can be a cheerleader for you, encouraging you to keep striving to be the best you can be.

Once you have your goals written down, you will begin to manage your boxes better. You'll start to value your time and energy, leading to more focus on the things that matter in life (spending more time in box 2).

Here's an additional exercise you can do—the Dream List. A dream is a little different from a goal, since it doesn't have a time limit, and can often just be a one-time thing. You can get really wild and crazy with your dream list—it can be anything you want to do in life.

Warning: be careful what you dream for—it probably will happen (since you wrote it down)!

<u>My dream list</u>

1.   6.

2.   7.

3.   8.

4.   9.

5.   10.

Below is an example of a dream list that I wrote fifteen years ago—I identify in parentheses "(done)" the dreams that have already come true;

<u>Bill's dream list</u>

1. Write a book (done)

2. See coliseum in Rome (done)

3. Visit Machu Picchu

4. Go to the top of the Eiffel Tower (done)

5. See the Taj Mahal (done)

6. Live/work overseas (done)

7. Work in TV/Radio (done)

8. Walk on the Great Wall of China (done)

9. Visit the Acropolis in Athens (done)

10. See the Pyramids in Egypt

So far, not bad—8 out of 10 dreams have come true. Maybe I need to write down some more.

Be sure to keep your dream list with your goal worksheet; you'll want to review it as time passes, to see what you've accomplished, and to add more things to the list.

So what does the Urgent/Important Matrix and goal setting have to do with our device/social media/Internet usage? Everything. Without good box management and goal setting we drift into empty activity.

As I mentioned in the previous chapter, we start out pretty well in life, with parents and teachers giving us direction. And then we grow up and life just sort of happens. The "perfect" plan unravels into a chaotic mishmash of events that we often feel control us. Life happens. But, we can mitigate the chaos by having some idea of which direction we wish to head in. It's up to you to lay out the road map you wish to follow—nobody else will do it for you, and nobody else should.

The quote at the beginning of this chapter, "Begin with the end in mind", comes from Stephen Covey's *The 7 Habits of Highly Effective People*. This idea encourages you to visualize where you want to be, and then structuring the plan to arrive at that destination.

Writing down your goals is a great start to moving your life in the right direction. Once you do this, you will see better box management and more proactive choices. If you combine goal setting with a conscious digital diet or fast for 30 days, you'll really begin to focus your time and energy on things that will change your attitude and outlook on life. You'll spend more time in Box 2.

Setting goals will not instantly turn your days into dream land. We still have to go to work, earn money to pay the rent and feed ourselves. But having goals will bring some peace and purpose to daily life. Instead of seeing daily life as a grind just to earn money—which leaves us prone to seeking digital distraction— goals provide a light at the end of the tunnel. The light is something to shoot for—like the stars. If you land on the moon, that's okay too; not many people have been to the moon.

Key Words

Seminar (n)—an educational or training session

Confidently (adv)—to be sure, comfortable in doing things

Depression (n)—feelings of sadness and hopelessness that last a long time

Frustration (n)—disappointment, upset about things

Cyber-universe (n)—the Internet, social media

Breaking out of (something) (idiom)—to change the way of doing things

Constructive (adj)—productive, meaningful

Misery (n)—a state of being very unhappy

Collaborate (v)—to work with others

Effective (adj)—works well, improves things

Convenient (adj)—easy to do or obtain

Periodically (adv)—a set period of time, a routine

Adjust (v)—to change, to improve

Handy (adj)—helpful, easy to access

Accountable (adj)—responsible to others and ourselves

Strive (v)—to work toward accomplishing something

Unravel (v)—to come loose, to fall apart

Chaotic (adj)—no order, confusing

Mishmash (n)—a collection of things that are out of order, don't make sense

Mitigate (v)—to lessen the effect of something

Visualize (v)—to imagine an outcome or future action

Proactive (adj)—to take action in a positive direction

Combine (v)—to put together two or more things

Diet (n)—a plan to reduce consumption, to consume less

Grind (n)—an unpleasant routine that keeps repeating

CEO's and email

What we're busy with is our choice; too often, we focus on the wrong things, leave other things undone and leave people hanging, creating vacuums. We have time for games, social media and videos, but we're too busy to respond to people.

Two of the busiest guys I ever met replied 90% of the time to my emails. Bill Amelio, the former CEO of Lenovo, and Jason Wang 王正新, the former CEO of Yuanta Financial, would send some reply, often just "Got it", "Thanks!" or ":)" to acknowledge my inquiries. If more information was required, they'd provide it.

Their secret? Handle emails once, and respect people. There's a reason they reached the level of CEO. They know the power of acknowledging people.

5

"Excuse me"

"Don't ask what the world needs. Ask what makes you come alive, and go do it. Because what the world needs is people who have come alive."

Howard Thurman

I'm on the MRT as it nears the Zhongxiao-Fuxing station. I can feel someone behind me, moving closer, then trying to maneuver between me and another person. Eventually, the young man squeezes through us, glancing at a string of LINE messages on his phone, as he readies to disembark.

All he had to say was "Excuse me" (對不起 , or 不好意思). But we don't do that anymore, we don't even speak the minimal amount of words that situations call for. It's not just on the MRT— it's in the MRT stations, department stores, sidewalks, on buses, at school, in coffee shops—we're losing our ability for the slightest courtesy—we don't speak. And we don't smile. **We just glance up and see people as obstacles in our path.**

We're preoccupied. It's the first, most basic consequence; our abandonment of simple courtesy toward others. As I walk along the underground mall between Zhongxiao-Fuxing and Zhongxiao-Dunhua, somewhere from 1/3 to 1/2 of the people are looking at their phones, texting or talking on their phones.

I call it the "Stagger-Stop-Stall Mall"; some of the HDs ("Head Downers") are slowed in their walk, almost staggering, others have stopped momentarily to type a text, and others have stalled, like a car that has run out of gas, stuck in place for minutes. It's a real-life video game for me as I dodge left and right to avoid contact with folks engrossed in whatever they're doing with their device.

These people can move out of my way

Whose responsibility is it to pay attention and avoid a collision? It seems selfish to ignore those around us as we move about the city; I'm getting tired of dodging people who aren't paying attention. Increasingly, folks are stopping everywhere and anywhere, often in the middle of sidewalks or hallways, forcing others to navigate around them. Shouldn't we at least step off to the side, out of the way of pedestrian traffic, rather than force others to alter their course?

The next time you're out and about the city, stop and notice how many people are using devices, only glancing up periodically as a navigational function--certainly not enough time to recognize anyone they might know--not engaging strangers or extending kindness. Plus, many have earphones in, adding a second layer of sensory interruption. Head down, glance up, look away, repeat, repeat, and repeat, as we multi-task our way through the day, avoiding contact with other humans.

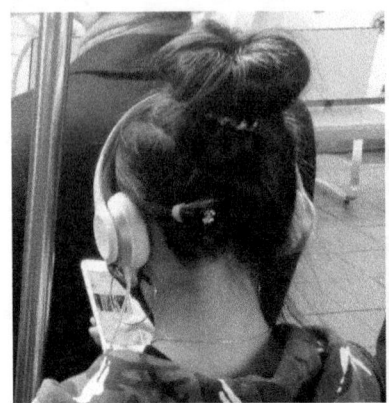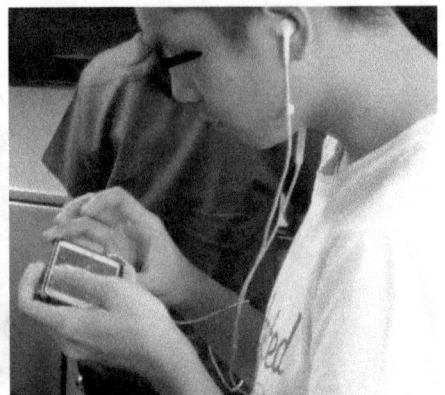

Tuning out the world, tuning out people

The occasional glances up from our phones remind me of some primitive behavior, looking out for predators that might eat us. These are the folks that are actually moving. Many people just stop, wherever they are, blocking walking lanes, not caring about forcing others to walk around them—not even realizing that others have to walk around them.

I'll just park my bike in the middle of this busy sidewalk

You go around me

I get it that Taipei is a busy, crowded city, and that we get tired of being surrounded by so many people, but I'm not sure that shutting out people is the best way to operate.

Does it matter? Should we care?

"Excuse me", "Hi", "Hello", "How are you?", "May I help you?", "Can you help me?" are the seeds of civility, the basic threads of relating with others.

These simple greetings and acknowledgments are the roots of conversation which may or may not lead to acquaintances or friendships, but do have a positive impact on our psychology and physiology. We feel less lonely, less isolated when we greet or are greeted and acknowledged by friends and strangers.

Studies have shown that serotonin levels in the brain are increased by simple acts of kindness, improving our moods. Three people benefit from even the simplest act of kindness: the person extending the kindness, the person receiving the kindness, and the person who observes the kindness. We're not kind to strangers like we used to be, and we all lose. Here's an article that summarizes how acts of kindness increase serotonin levels and improve moods;

The mass avoidance of interpersonal contact and civility at even the most basic level shortchanges society of thousands of moments each day that could have a positive impact on the collective psyche of society.

I'm lonely

I'm a social person, but as technology overtakes us I experience fewer "contacts" with people each day—far less than I experienced here ten years ago. I like to say "Hello" to people and acknowledge them. But it's difficult to do when so few people are available for even eye contact, let alone a verbal greeting. I know I'm not the only person who is lonely.

Occasionally, when people do look, say hello and talk for a few moments, most of the time they smile and their faces light up. I've even had some people ask me for a hug! These are people that I just met a few minutes before! So, I hug them (who knows how many years it's been since their last hug). If I can bring a little sunshine to somebody's life it makes me feel better too. But far too many of us walk around, sealing off others, being stoic, denying our loneliness, and blocking any escape route out of our isolation.

Here's an example of how being available can create serendipitous moments: Recently I was at the bus stop near my apartment, just waiting (almost everybody was looking at their phone). I noticed that a guy near me (not looking at a phone) had on a Dallas Mavericks shirt. So I asked him if that was his favorite NBA team. Andy Lu enthusiastically replied that he loved the Mavericks, and then we had a nice three-minute conversation.

Andy Lu 盧雍凱 . . .

. . . and the bus stop where we met

In three minutes I learned much about him. He's typical of most people in Taiwan—friendly, pleasant and bright—but the difference was that he was present in the moment and available for a conversation. I wished this happened more often. When's the last time you met somebody at the bus stop?

Sadly, talking to people we don't know almost seems strange these days

Lonely in a crowded city that has everything

Why are so many people in Taiwan depressed, frustrated, and melancholic? We have everything—EVERYTHING—yet discontent pervades. Maybe a little gratitude for our blessings would help. We have a healthcare system the world envies, a transportation system that is amazingly efficient, endless entertainment options, economic stability and prosperity, freedom, plentiful food and water, and most importantly, peace (think of all the nations at war).

Yet an undertone of discontent flows within many of us. So we scroll and scroll and scroll, in search of a solution in the palm of our hands, hoping that somebody cares, measuring our worth in the number of "likes" we receive on Facebook. And more focused on capturing Pokémon than building relationships with new people that may create real change in our lives.

I've seen basic civility work—it can be transformative. My job with Studio Classroom put me in a unique position to engage others. Many people in Taiwan are familiar with Studio Classroom, and thanks to my years on the Advanced Magazine radio program I have plenty of things to talk about with strangers. Over the years I've made it a habit to greet people—yes, people I don't know—in everyday situations. It's amazing what a simple "Hi, how are you?" or "How's it going?" can do—in many cases they're stunned that somebody is even talking to them.

From many of these greetings have sprung brief conversations—maybe they only last 30 or 60 seconds—but the change it creates in them *and* me is remarkable. People like to be acknowledged, they appreciate even a few moments of care. I've lost track of how many students I've met who were in a bad mood, exhausted, frustrated—and within a minute were smiling and laughing, because instead of looking at my phone, I looked at them, smiled and said "Hi". That's called a win-win.

You might think "Well, that's all fine and dandy for you, Bill", but I know that you too can do the same. Instead of looking at your phone, look for opportunities to be a ray of light in someone's life. It'll be good for everybody. Civility leads to community, community leads to compassion, and compassion leads to enrichment. Right now, we're aborting this process before it ever begins because we avoid eye contact. We think clicking on "Like" is a satisfactory expression of empathy, and then we move on to other posts. We've forgotten that real civility, compassion and empathy require effort, time and thought.

It is true that we can find communities on social media, but I've found that it narrows my focus only to people I like or things I'm interested in. The term for this is "echo chambers".

For me to truly grow, I need to step outside of my comfort zone, to flavor the good, the bad and the ugly in life; to deal with people who don't look like me, don't think like me, and don't share the same experiences. If I just limit myself to my social media circles (my echo chambers), scrolling Facebook or LINE, watching videos or playing games, then I block out the real people that I encounter every day who God has put there to teach me something.

In the bible there are countless examples of Jesus meeting people along the way—He was going somewhere, encountered a person, and then performed a miracle, taught a lesson, and transformed a life. Imagine Jesus walking past the poor and downtrodden, busy looking at his phone, earphones in listening to music, not hearing those people or acknowledging their pleas;

You too can do miracles—you don't have to look for them; those opportunities will find you. You just have to be available.

Key Words

Maneuver (v)—to move, to adjust course

Disembark (v)—to get off a plane, train or ship

Obstacle (n)—something that blocks our way

Preoccupied (adj)—busy with something else

Abandonment (n)—the act of giving up something

Stagger (v)—to walk in a way that is not straight

Stall (v)—to slow down, a lack of power

Dodge (v)—to move quickly to avoid something

Engrossed in (idiom)—to give all your attention to something

Collision (n)—two objects running into each other

Pedestrian (n)—a person walking on a street or sidewalk

Alter (v)—to change, adjust

Function (n)—how something works

Extend (v)—to give

Sensory (adj)—seeing, hearing, smelling things

Interruption (n)—something that is unplanned, takes our attention away

Multi-task (v)—doing two or more things at the same time

Predator (n)—a human or animal that hunts other beings, usually as food

Get it (figure of speech)—to understand something

Civility (n)—the act of treating others with respect

Acquaintance (n)—someone we know

Physiology (n)—our physical state

Serotonin (n)—a chemical that affects our mood

Available (adj)—able to attend, be present or help

Sealing off (v ph)—to shut out something, make it not possible

Stoic (adj)—showing little or no emotion

Isolation (n)—being alone, separated from others for long periods of time

Enthusiastically (adv)—to do something with energy and excitement

Typical (adj)—common, similar

Present in the moment (figure of speech)—to be fully conscious, paying attention

Melancholic (adj)—sad, depressed, little energy

Discontent (n)—not pleased or satisfied with things

Pervades (v)—to exist in all parts, all places

Gratitude (n)—being thankful for things

Envy (v)—to be jealous of others

Prosperity (n)—good economic status

Undertone (n)—a hidden reason or theme

Unique (adj)—special, different

Stunned (adj)—very surprised

Sprung (v)—to rise up quickly

Lose track (idiom)—to forget something, not remember exactly

Win-win (n)—two people benefit at the same time

Compassion (n)—kindness, care, help

Enrichment (n)—something that makes us better

Empathy (n)—understanding what others are feeling or experiencing, showing care

Narrow (v)—to reduce or limit something

Echo chamber (n)—a group of people that only agree

Comfort zone (n)—a feeling of no stress, a familiar place

Block out (v ph)—to prevent something from happening

Encounter (v)—to meet another person or experience

Downtrodden (n)—sick or less fortunate people

6

Non-stop availability

"And what I've found is that our little devices, those little devices in our pockets, are so psychologically powerful that they don't only change what we do, they change who we are."

Sherry Turkle

900 Facebook friends. Many that I've never met in person.

What is the purpose of this? To expand my network? Some people I know have 2,000 or 3,000 or more Facebook friends (a more accurate term would be "acquaintances"). And we all have "friends" around the world, on Facebook, LINE and many other platforms. (Is it necessary to be friends with everybody forever?) I now get messages and comments 24/7. People want to have digital conversations with me at 5am, 6pm, noon and midnight. It never stops. And if you're on LINE or Twitter, the deluge is multiplied.

At 7 pm on a Tuesday evening I was going over a lesson with one of my tutoring students, Phillip, a high level banking executive. For most of the lesson his phone kept beeping and lighting up. He kept glancing over at it, and I couldn't help but look at it also—the phone was beckoning us!

He belongs to ten LINE groups, involving about 100 people. Ding, ding, ding; light, light, light. Eventually he muted the sound, but the light continued. It was interrupting our lesson, so I asked Phillip what the messages were about.

"Nothing important" he said. A couple jokes, some dinner plans, a few personal questions, all generating posts by group members—the LINE groups were going full-bore—and we kept getting interrupted by "nothing important". This was just one hour in his day. I multiplied that hour by the number of hours he's awake, then looked out at the department he supervises—about 80 employees, all with phones, all on LINE and Facebook—and imagined the digital cacophony that swamps that group in a single day. It's amazing that anything gets done.

Do our devices and social media make us more productive? We convince ourselves they do, without ever analyzing it. But are we really more productive, or just busy?

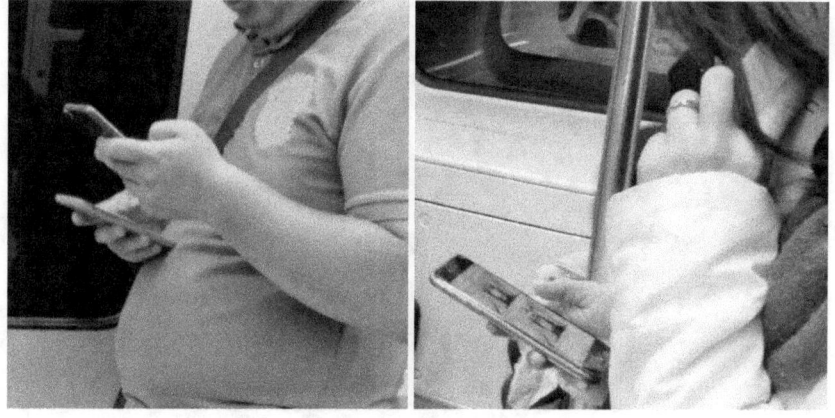

Dueling phones: We're very busy—but are we productive?

Multiple studies over the past several decades have shown that workers in a typical 8 hour work day are productive 50% of the time. Now, we've added all of these digital distractions. My guess is that we're not more productive—but I'm pretty sure that we're more stressed out.

We're trying to get our work done and have added to the mix a cornucopia of "nothing important", which stealthily sucks time and drains our mental and emotional batteries.

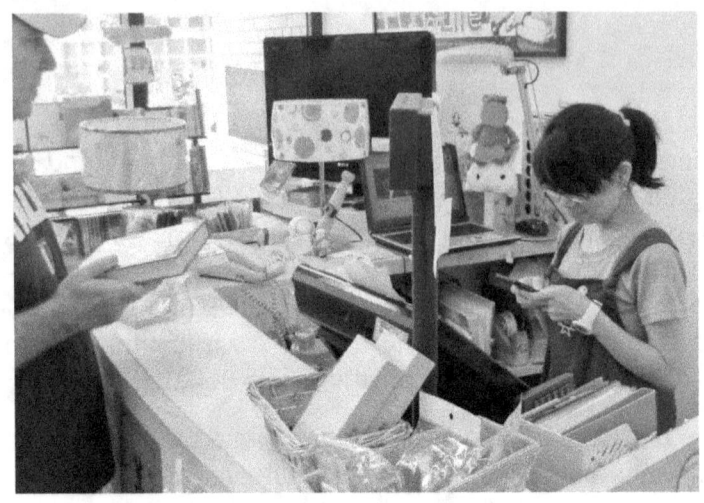

In the workplace . . . at the office

And now, thanks to technology that's always on and on us, we have the curse of all employees—the supervisor who knows no boundaries and uses social media to send messages to the staff around the clock, 7 days a week—with the expectation of an immediate reply.

These supervisory LINE, WhatsApp, WeChat and text messages can fall into the categories of "Very important", "Kind of important", or "Not important". But here's the problem—**we have**

to process all messages, which takes time and attention, whether they are from the boss or family or friends, because without processing them we might miss the few things that are important.

And process we do! Consider how many digital platforms that hundreds, maybe thousands of people can contact you with; email, LINE, Facebook, LinkedIn, Skype, WhatsApp, WeChat, Twitter, Viber, Instagram, etc. In a day, we may get hundreds of emails, texts, messages, voicemails and comments. Some of these have attachments to read, videos to watch, links to click on, responses that are required—leading to more, more, more. Without understanding what we were wading into, **we've become information processors**.

Everywhere we go we look at screens—constantly.

The paradox is that we miss so much.

One for the wife, one for the girlfriend?

Ironically, even with all of our digital communicating, few of us are "experts" at it. We may be quick—sometimes—but digital communications is often incomplete, full of misunderstanding. And in our haste, we sometimes make mistakes. Did you ever quickly send an email, text, LINE or FB message and then soon regret it? Our rush to reply doesn't leave time to ponder how best to reply, especially when we're angry or emotional.

We should have classes in schools that teach teens how to graciously communicate digitally. For instance, I teach a 12-week corporate course just on email—how to write effective emails for a variety of purposes. That's twelve lessons just on email! Digital communicating requires a certain "touch", particularly since it's a one-way method of communicating, rather than a dialogue that flows.

Many of us are drowning in this ocean of digital commotion, devoting time to processing, replying, posting and commenting, liking and sharing, mostly with mere acquaintances, while cutting back on phone calls and conversations with the folks nearest and dearest to us.

So, let's take a look at the Urgent/Important matrix as it relates to our digital activity. Our digital activity has become so

prominent in our lives that we need to analyze how it breaks down. Here is an example;

High	**Urgency**	Low

1. Urgent and Important (Do it now) A. Messages from the boss B. Important emails C. Work related messages	2. Not Urgent and Important (Plan) A. PowerPoints for work B. Customer proposals C. Digital platform marketing
3. Urgent and Not Important (Avoid if possible) A. Posting pictures on FB B. LINE (social) conversations C. Non-work related emails	4. Not Urgent and Not Important (Low priority) A. Games B. Watching videos C. Gossip

Importance (vertical axis, High to Low)

Digital Activity

Over the past 13 years I've taught people from all walks of life: students, teachers, business executives, waiters and waitresses, taxi drivers, etc., at all different levels of ability. One thing that is **consistent**: the people who make 10,000,000 to 30,000,000 NT$/year do not **hang out** in box 3 (Urgent, Not Important). Their phones are tools, not **crutches**. They know when to put it down—because they understand how important their time and mental energy is. Their time is money. Their mental energy is targeted wisely. They hang out in box 2.

In fact, successful people are very precise about minutes devoted to activities. That's one difference between those who reach goals vs. those that drift; minutes matter to the successful.

Do your minutes matter?

Now, you fill in this Digital Activity matrix with your daily digital routine;

High	Urgency	Low
1. Urgent and Important (Do it now) A. B. C.		2. Not Urgent and Important (Plan) A. B. C.
3. Urgent and Not Important (Avoid if possible) A. B. C.		4. Not Urgent and Not Important (Low priority) A. B. C.

Importance — High (top), Low (bottom)

Your Digital Activity

If we added up the time spent every day in boxes 3 and 4 we'd be surprised. The key to achieving our goals in life is to shift as much time as possible to box 2, because Boxes 3 and 4 are getting in the way. It's all about the choices you make with your discretionary time—those free periods of time in which you choose what to do. Sadly, most people bounce between Boxes 1 and 3, putting out fires in Box 1, then drifting in Box 3, wasting discretionary time on things that don't matter. (Spending discretionary time in Boxes 3 and 4 during the day is also why you're not getting enough sleep at night, which I cover in chapter 15.)

Is it necessary for me to be in a state of non-stop availability?

Sherry Turkle, a psychologist and researcher at MIT who has spent 30 years studying the impact of mobile devices and social media on people, gave one of the best TED Talks that I've seen, titled "Connected, but alone?" She speaks about this "always on, always on us" phenomenon, and how it alters our life. I strongly suggest you watch it. (Chinese subtitles are available on most TED Talks);

Yes, we're busy, but we need to do some critical thinking about our "busy". We may feel like information processors, but you can do something about it—you can reign it in and take control of your life. It doesn't require a drastic change, just some fine-tuning of your digital M.O.

Helpful tip

Take time to understand the difference between the words busy, productive and constructive. We can be busy, but not get a lot of the important things done. We can be productive, getting things done, but often not leading to the next step in our progress. We must step back and analyze if our busyness and productivity are constructive, helping to create a better future. Apply these words to the activities you choose to devote energy to, and steer your energy to the constructive activities.

Key Words

Network (n)—the large group of people that I am connected with

Accurate (adj)—exact, precise

Multiply (v)—to make larger by doubling or tripling (or more)

Beckon (v)—to call, to ask someone to come

Mute (v)—to silence

Going full-bore (figure of speech)—moving at a high speed or volume

Cacophony (n)—a collection of noise with no order

Swamp (v)—to flood or overwhelm, too much

Stressed out (idiom)—feeling mental and emotional strain

Cornucopia (n)—a large variety of things

Stealthily (adv)—doing something without being noticed

Curse (n)—a wish of bad luck, a burden

Boundaries (n)—limits, guidelines

Expectation (n)—expecting something to happen

Attachment (n)—a document or file that is added to an email or message

Wading into (idiom)—slowly moving into something that is usually unknown

Ironically (adv)—two things that seem alike but are actually opposite

Haste (n)—rushing, doing something too quickly

Regret (n)—feeling bad about something that was done or said

Ponder (v)—to think about something, contemplate

Graciously (adv)—doing something with kindness and care

Touch (n)—skill, a special ability

Particularly (adv)—specifically, special attention to something

Dialogue (n)—two people having a conversation

Commotion (n)—a disturbance, something unplanned and not organized

Cut back (idiom)—to reduce something

Prominent (adj)—very important, famous or notable

Consistent (adj)—doing the same thing most of the time, regular

Hang out (idiom)—to spend time somewhere

Crutch (n)—a tool to help people to walk, a support

Getting in the way (figure of speech)—preventing something or other things from happening

Discretionary (adj)—having a choice, using judgement

Putting out fires (figure of speech)—handling emergencies, solving problems

Phenomenon (n)—a unique thing or set of circumstances

Reign (something) in (idiom)—to control or limit something

M.O. (mode of operation) (n)—how you operate or function

7

"There's more to life than increasing its speed"

Mahatma Gandhi

Another serious consequence of our head-down behavior is that the roads are less safe.

Sitting in the back seat of a taxi, rolling along Minquan Road, near Songshan Airport, I look out the window to my left and see a guy riding a scooter, steering with his right hand, and holding his phone to his ear with his left hand. We move ahead of him, and I'm able to snap this picture;

What is so important that he would risk serious injury or possibly death?

It's a fairly common scene in Taipei, motorcycle riders talking on the phone, or even texting, while driving, which creates a triple threat that is overlooked, ignored or even joked about—but it's no laughing matter. It's dangerous for three reasons;

66

- His ability to steer his motorcycle is greatly impaired
- His cognitive ability to assess and react to traffic situations is greatly impaired
- He's a danger to other motorcycle riders, pedestrians and even cars. If he swerves or hits a bump in the road and loses control, then other vehicles would react, causing them to possibly hit someone

All because he can't resist multi-tasking with his phone. As we know, death or serious injury to riders and pedestrians can happen in the blink of an eye. **What is this** mental block **that we've been** seduced **into?** Most accidents are due to operator error; our distraction behavior has increased the danger. We might think "I'm not bothering anybody", but actually we're endangering others.

Once, I was riding my bicycle on Ren Ai Road, and a young lady went past me on her scooter, holding a phone with her left hand to her right ear—essentially crossing her arm over her body—driving with one hand, weaving along at erratic speeds. At the next red light I pulled up to her—she was still in conversation on her phone—and told her that this behavior was very dangerous. She just quickly looked at me, nodded, and continued her conversation. She didn't want to be interrupted, and seemed upset that I said something to her about this behavior being dangerous. She didn't understand that she was not only putting herself at risk, but others as well. The light turned green and she drove off, still talking on the phone.

We underestimate the importance of concentration when moving about.

Then there are cars. In America there has been much media coverage of drivers who have killed or maimed people due to texting or talking on the phone while driving, but I haven't seen much about this in the media here in Taiwan. **In fact, talking and texting while driving have been compared to drunk driving;**

<u>Driving distracted</u>

I know this problem exists in Taiwan because daily I ride my bicycle around Taipei, and have had some close calls with drivers who were enraptured in phone calls or texting while driving. Sometimes they run red lights, sometimes they blindly make turns at intersections, sometimes they drift in their lanes as they look down at their phones. I've been told that it's against the law to use your phone while driving, but I've never seen it enforced.

Even if the police enforced the "no phone while driving" laws, I don't think this behavior would decline. We've become so accustomed to using our phones while driving that no amount of fines would deter us. (I've also had near misses on my bike with people walking out in front of me, looking at their phones, and even had close calls with other bike riders who are talking or texting on their phones!)

One of the great secrets of Taipei is just how many people are driving and using their phones. When I ride my bike, I'm able to maneuver among traffic at intersections, and observe drivers. I can tell you that at least 1/3 of the drivers I observe are using their phones—talking, texting, listening to/leaving WeChat voice messages, watching videos, etc. Why is this a secret? Because almost every car in Taipei has darkly tinted windows—you can't see inside unless you get really close to the cars.

Here's a video of distracted driving (from Kaohsiung);

There are probably more accidents that happen due to phone distraction than we will ever know about. Most people will never admit they caused an accident because they were busy with their phone. Only by tracing call and text records do we find out.

It's scary to think of how many people are rolling around this city at any moment, not paying full attention to what they are doing. We've decided that driving is a great time for multi-tasking, and are able to avoid the law with our stealth windows. And yet, the danger is ignored—drivers ignore the risk, and the media ignores it. That's why you need to pay attention as a pedestrian—because many of the drivers aren't paying attention.

Here's a link to the Center for Disease Control in America, which covers "Distracted Driving Deaths";

From the CDC website I pulled this;

What are the types of distraction?

There are three main types of distraction:

- Visual: taking your eyes off the road;
- Manual: taking your hands off the wheel; and
- Cognitive: taking your mind off of driving.

Distracted driving activities

Distracted driving activities include things like using a cell phone, texting, and eating. Using in-vehicle technologies (such as navigation systems) can also be sources of distraction. While any of these distractions can endanger the driver and others, texting while driving is especially dangerous because it combines all three types of distraction.

Every day in America 8 people are killed due to distracted driving. It's estimated that 25% of teen drivers are texting while driving. How many distracted driving deaths are there in Taiwan each year? It's hard to find data on this, specifically for Taiwan. But several studies have shown dramatic increases around the globe, so, it's likely that Taiwan follows this trend. This article states "Distracted driving is a growing public safety hazard";

We're not taking this stuff seriously enough—we're ignoring the problem, at our own peril. We think "it will happen to someone else". These are unnecessary deaths and injuries, all because we're selfish: we can't wait and we aren't paying attention. We're maiming and killing innocent people, collectively shrugging our shoulders and looking the other way.

These drivers using their phone have been reduced to one-hand drivers; the other hand is holding the phone as they talk or worse, text. It results in sensory degradation—less ability to drive the car.

One-hand driving also means turn signals are used less frequently—often not used at all—so pedestrians and other vehicles don't know if the driver will turn. And vision is affected because of the distraction—texting is the worst.

The driver ability degradation is particularly profound at intersections, such as left turns right in front of motorcycles that the driver doesn't see coming, or right turns done in a rush, that endanger pedestrians crossing the street. In both cases one hand driving, no turn signal and vision impairment are major problems. And "hands-free" driving—using a holder for your device—is dangerous also, as this National Safety Council article explains.

Even digital activity while sitting at intersections can degrade our driving ability. We momentarily check out of the situation, and the text messages we send often generate replies that occur while we're driving, **triggering** a sensory and physical response that can distract us.

This "multi-media" taxi had me feeling a little nervous. (And taxi drivers always answer their phones when driving, which is a safety issue.)

But we're all super-intelligent creatures, capable of multi-tasking at high quality levels, right? That's what we think . . . until our accident happens, and then we pay the price of our carelessness.

Here's an article with 10 statistics on distracted driving in the U.S., such as 1 in 4 accidents involve a cellphone—I'm confident that similar statistics can be applied to Taiwan;

Earlier this year I was riding on a bus in downtown Taipei. There were about ten passengers, and I was seated near the front. To my amazement, the driver started watching a video on his phone! Not only was he watching it at a red light, but he continued to watch the video, phone in his left hand, and driving! This is a great example of how we've become lulled into "It's okay, it's not a problem";

Here's the video I took of this distracted bus driver:

What is so important that we must use the phones while driving?

<u>People walking, talking and texting—but not looking</u>

This brings us to the third party in the digitally dangerous road scenario—pedestrians. I'm stunned at how many pedestrians obliviously walk (usually at a slower, distracted pace) across streets, hypnotized by their phones, not looking in any direction to make sure that it is safe, having conversations with some distant person, ignoring their perimeter, naively assuming that drivers will stop.

BREAKING NEWS **FOR PEDESTRIANS: Not all drivers are having a good day.**

A few are drunk (and maybe using their phone), while some are speeding, running red lights, and making illegal turns.

In addition to looking only at the phone while crossing streets, earphones will often be in, reducing or eliminating the ability to hear oncoming trouble. This double sensory interruption makes pedestrians particularly vulnerable to drivers who are making turns at busy intersections. I never use earphones while riding my bike or walking around Taipei: **it's necessary for me to hear what is happening around me**, especially people, bicycles, motorcycles or vehicles coming from behind.

Pedestrian looking at tablet as car approaches

One other pedestrian risk that we can see every day are the people waiting at busy, high-speed intersections, standing **perilously** close to moving traffic, not looking at the traffic, but looking at their phones. Why take that chance? There are dangerous drivers in every city—always have been—but we're **compounding** the situation with collective distraction. We're multiplying our **blind spots** with visual and audio distraction.

You could say that Taipei has a "perfect storm" of factors that endangers all of us on the streets: high-density traffic, aggressive drivers with a "me first" approach, lax enforcement of traffic laws (especially no enforcement of "talking/texting while driving laws"), digitally distracted drivers and pedestrians looking at devices.

It's all about awareness **of surroundings.** I realize it's impossible to be vigilant every moment of the day, scanning our surroundings for pending danger; we don't want to go through life on the edge. But we also don't want to completely disregard what's going on around us. **If I'm constantly distracted then my** alertness **is** compromised. Most of the time that's okay, but the likelihood of a collision, whether with vehicles or other pedestrians, has increased since a significant percentage of people are distracted.

This guy wandered through the middle of the extremely busy Minsheng-Dunhua intersection, looking at his phone.

Awareness

Degraded alertness also comes into play in emergency situations. Recently I was near an MRT escalator at the Chungshiao-Dunhua station, and a little girl's shoelace got stuck in the top of the escalator—it started to pull her shoe off, and there was a risk of her foot being injured. Around this area were people, ten feet away, looking at their phones, completely unaware of what was happening. Her mother frantically tried to get her shoe free from the escalator—and people kept walking past. I was about thirty feet away, and ran over to push the emergency stop button, but fortunately her mother was able to free the shoe from the still running escalator. It all happened in a matter of seconds.

On the MRT a few years ago we had the terrible incident of the young man stabbing people, resulting in four deaths. I wondered if people were looking at their devices when this incident started, and if awareness of surroundings may have prevented some of the injuries and deaths.

Consider this: In San Francisco there was an incident on their subway where a man pulled out a gun a couple times while people concentrated on their phones—he was waving the gun around, pointing it at people. Nobody noticed. Eventually he shot and killed one of the passengers.

Here's a link to the article about the San Francisco shooting;

We can't assume that someone else will handle emergency situations—it's up to all of us to be prepared and be alert. So, keep your eyes open, observe who's around you; don't just bury yourself in the device for extended periods of time, completely unaware of your surroundings.

Have you ever read the instructions on these items below? Would you know how to use them? In emergency situations sometimes a few seconds can make a huge difference.

The next time you're on a bus or the MRT, look up from the phone and study these items. The fire extinguisher could have been used as a weapon against the MRT murderer, by spraying it at him. Or, in the tragic bus fire that killed 26 people near Taoyuan, it could have been used to break one of the windows (by hitting the bottom against a corner of a window). It's likely that many of the tourists on that bus used their phones while riding, but unlikely that anybody checked to see where the extinguisher was. Awareness may have saved a couple lives.

"Situational awareness" isn't just for emergencies. While theft isn't a major concern here in Taiwan, we can't take that for granted when traveling overseas. While visiting the Louvre in Paris, a close friend of mine was scrolling through some messages on her phone, as she waited to enter the museum. When she looked at her purse, she realized that the latch had been undone, and then discovered that 80 Euros had been taken from her purse. Heads up; there are professional pick-pockets just waiting for tourists to not pay attention.

My friend Phil, who is a teacher in Anshan, China, shared with me that one of his students was sitting in a park, set her purse down on the bench, and while she and a friend were looking at some photos on her phone, a thief came by and stole her purse (maybe the thief noticed they weren't paying attention).

In Taiwan we can be lulled into a sense of security here, since crime is not so rampant. What happens then is we continue our behavior on our journeys, not being vigilant in foreign settings, and continuing to look at our devices. I certainly don't want to discourage people from traveling abroad—we just can't be careless or too distracted.

We can't be too careless here in Taipei, either. Many times late at night I'll be walking along and come across other people walking in the dark, looking at their phones, not paying attention to their surroundings. This is particularly important for women, whom I will often see looking down for long periods of time as they walk along dark streets or sidewalks—unaware of people around them that might be threats.

Here are two photos (next page) that I took at 10 pm the second night after a young child was viciously killed by a drug-crazed lunatic in Neihu—both people had no idea I was standing there, taking pictures as they staggered along, oblivious to their surroundings.

Focused too much on phones, not surroundings

We don't want to be paranoid as we walk around town, but oddly, the stabbings on the MRT and the murder in Neihu did nothing to change our behavior regarding situational awareness. Within days we return to myopic behavior. A little sensibility could go a long way toward preventing potential problems.

Helpful reminders

1. Decide before getting in a car or on your motorcycle to not talk or text while driving. Put the phone in a compartment.

2. Decide not to talk, text or look at phone while crossing or near busy streets and intersections.

3. Be aware of the importance of hearing your surroundings.

4. Check out surroundings for exits, emergency equipment and alarms (on MRT, buses, unfamiliar places).

5. Be aware of surroundings and people, especially at night.

Key Words

Overlook (v)—to not see or notice, not pay attention

Impair (v)—to lower the quality of something, to prevent

Cognitive (adj)—thought process, thinking, mental ability

Assess (v)—to evaluate, measure

Swerve (v)—to suddenly move to a side

In the blink of an eye (figure of speech)—to happen very, very quickly

Mental block (n ph)—something that prevents us from thinking about an issue

Seduce (v)—to persuade, to be lured into something

Weave (v)—moving left and right as we move forward

Erratic (adj)—not consistent, unpredictable

Underestimate (v)—to not know the full value or meaning of something

Concentration (n)—apply mental ability and attention

Maim (v)—to seriously injure

Close call (n ph)—a near miss, almost an accident

Enraptured (adj)—totally focused on something, lost in thought

Enforce (v)—to apply a rule or law

Accustomed to (v ph)—used to something, comfortable

Deter (v)—to discourage an action or activity

Observe (v)—to watch, see

Tinted (adj)—dark shading that is applied to windows to block sunlight

Estimate (v)—to provide an approximate number based on known information

Peril (n)—danger, risk

Selfish (adj)—thinking only of the self

Degradation (n)—a lowering of quality

Turn signal (n)—the lights on a vehicle that indicate the vehicle will turn

Profound (adj)—very important and meaningful

Trigger (v)—to cause something to happen

Carelessness (n)—not caring, not paying attention

Amazement (n)—total surprise, unexpected

Party (n)—a person or group in a situation

Scenario (n)—a situation

Obliviously (adv)—unaware of things nearby

Hypnotized (adj)—not fully conscious or aware of reality

Perimeter (n)—the area all around us, nearby

Naively (adv)—not wise, ignorant of reality

Assume (v)—thinking something is true or will happen without knowing for sure

Breaking news (n ph)—fresh information, aimed at getting attention

Eliminate (v)—to get rid of something

Oncoming (adj)—something coming toward us

Vulnerable (adj)—in danger, easily hurt

Perilously (adv)—dangerous, risky

Compound (v)—to make something worse

Blind spot (n)—something that prevents us from seeing, hearing or thinking

Perfect storm (n ph)—a combination of bad things that come together at the same time

High-density (adj)—very crowded

Aggressive (adj)—acting in a way that is fast, forceful, not careful

Lax (adj)—not strong, weak

Awareness (n)—knowing what is happening

Vigilant (adj)—determined, on watch

Scan (v)—to quickly look around, searching for something

Pending (adj)—something that will or possibly could happen

On the edge (figure of speech)—very alert, a state of being tense, not relaxed

Disregard (v)—to determine that something isn't important

Alertness (n)—being aware, watching or listening for danger

Compromised (v)—a weakened position

Likelihood (n)—the possibility of something happening

Frantically (adv)—excited, worried or nervous movement

Incident (n)—something that happens

Extended period (n)—a long period of time

Situational (adj)—the present place or situation that we are in

Take (something) for granted (idiom)—to not fully value something

Pick-pocket (n)—a person that steals money or wallets from people in a sneaky way

A sense of security (n ph)—feeling comfortable, safe

Rampant (adj)—often, frequent, widespread

Viciously (adv)—violent, brutal

Drug-crazed (adj)—strongly influenced by drugs, unpredictable behavior

Lunatic (n)—a crazy person

Paranoid (adj)—fearing almost everything and everybody

Myopic (adj)—unable to act wisely, short-sighted

Sensibility (n)—using logic, common sense, making good choices

8

Love and Technology

"When you are content to simply be yourself and don't compare or compete, everybody will respect you."

Lao Tzu

An ancient American proverb:

"She married the perfect man, then spent the next ten years fixing him."

If you think you're going to change somebody's behavior, be ready for years of frustration. They have to want to change, and it will be on their schedule.

I'm trying to get a grip on how the head-down behavior affects mating. I wonder if young men are learning how to treat young women in ways that please the ladies. Or maybe the guys are focusing too much on their phones and games, instead of delving into the mysteries of relating. Over the past five years in Taipei I've noticed a dramatic increase in the number of young women (18-25) who have female partners. If they're happy, then I'm happy for them; it's human nature to seek connection, attention, approval and intimacy.

Holding hands is better than holding phones

I don't know what percentage of young women are truly lesbians—there seems to be a facet of exploration involved—but in my conversations with many young women, one theme frequently comes up; they're frustrated that so many of the young men are preoccupied with video games, and that **finding a truly motivated young man (i.e. work, career, goals, possibly interested in children) who is attentive to their needs is difficult.**

Whether a young person pursues a lesbian or gay relationship is either their predisposition or choice, and it really doesn't matter to me which path they follow. (As a Christian, I'd like to see traditional marriages, but God gives us freedom of choice.) What is apparent to me is that young women seek companionship, and they are addressing that in different ways. So, I wonder if excessive gaming gets in the way of romance.

*Note for women who may be tempted to settle with a serious gamer: marriage will not make that behavior go away—it needs to be dealt with prior to marriage.

*Note for guys: cut back on the gaming and Internet surfing, and pay more attention to the super women around you.

Diversions and interference

Internet porn is another diversion for men, so we also need to ask if this is blocking young men from relating to women. I haven't seen this issue get much attention here in Taiwan, but it's real and exists everywhere in the world, so we're naïve to think that it's not an issue here.

Even when couples do marry, serious digital interference still exists. I've spoken with many wives with children who've told me that their husbands stare at the computer screen all night while she takes care of the kids. I've also known men who stay late at the office, using devices, games and social media to avoid being husbands and parents. Excessive gaming prevents intimate communication, drains energy and sucks the life out of a relationship. (Note: women spend a lot of times on games, too, so it's not just a guy problem.)

If we're devoting significant time to gaming, that's time and attention we're withholding from our partners and children. And many online games are violent, numbing our sensitivities, or show women as sexual objects, skewing male perceptions of females.

Future husbands

Be a smart shopper

We need to examine how phones, tablets, the Internet and social media have altered our meeting and mating processes—I'm not sure the impact has been entirely positive. New avenues of meeting people have opened up, such as singles websites, online groups that share activity and lifestyle interests, and the ability to meet interesting people online from other countries and continents. The world has become our marketplace for mating, and that's okay—but we need to be wise about this.

Do diligent research, because a Pandora's Box of relational pitfalls has sprung loose in cyberspace.

Digital representations of people can be misleading and/or inaccurate, sometimes hiding critical issues. Before all of this digital chasing, we usually met people in person; in school, at work, through friends or chance encounters—and we usually knew more about the people we met. Now, we hang out in the digital-mating shopping mall—an online meat-market, with far more people involved in the process—because it's so easy to contact and entertain large numbers of suitors and prospects. It's quite common for people who are "in the market" for a mate to be flirting with dozens of people, all around the world—leading to lots of misrepresentation.

(Oddly, once many couples do connect, they switch into a form of digital monitoring—the constant text messages, calls and Facebook checks that smother the other person. Couples used to spend time apart, maybe missing the other person, but now our phones keep us tethered to the other person 24/7.)

A female friend of mine once told me that she had 47 guys on Match.com sending her messages, trying to meet her, just at that moment in time. Is that really a better way? We reduce prospective mates to attractive images and semi-fictitious profiles, then act surprised when they're not what we thought they were. I've also known of men (from North America and Europe) who go on Asian tours after meeting several women online, arranging stops in various countries in a sort of recruiting trip. My close friend Sherry had this experience;

Sherry, worked here in Taipei. Online she met Jack, a 24-year-old U.S. Army soldier from Iowa. His profile looked great; very impressive photos in uniform, muscular, handsome. He was on duty in Afghanistan, and they exchanged the usual messages that people do. On a leave from Afghanistan, he made plans to visit Sherry in Taipei. They ended up spending a few days hanging out at the hotel he was staying at, with much of the time in bed. During this get-together, Sherry discovered (through phone calls she heard and text messages she saw) that Jack was then flying on to Manila, to meet up with a couple of other women he met online, and then on to Bangkok to meet a couple more. He had arranged a two-week Southeast Asian tour of women he met online. Sherry learned the hard way that great profiles often disguise questionable character and integrity.

Be careful.

Or maybe you've had this experience of being the victim of lying by omission, which my friend James shared;

"The next woman I attempted to get to know was long distance and extremely inconsistent. She was telling me that she could see us getting married, but she could never find time for me to actually come visit her. As an April Fools' Day joke I suggested that we both announce on Facebook that we were engaged to each other. Ha ha. That's when she informed me that she WAS already engaged! Ha ha ha....ha. Joke's on me!"

Rushing into things, then disappearing

We've "evolved" to where some people think it's okay to mess with people like James—they're distant and disposable. Another consequence of digital mating has been "ghosting"—the technique of digitally disappearing from relationships. I think the reason for the increase in ghosting is that we're trying to deal with too many people online, rush into things, then instead of ending things in mature ways, the easy way out is to just disappear—which adds to our online angst.

Ghosting isn't limited to romantic communications; it infects friendships and business communications. It's an easy way out. Rather than going through conflict resolution, we digitally run and hide—which usually causes permanent damage to the relationship. Then we're left with a trail of people we try to avoid for the rest of our lives, playing a digital form of "hide and seek". While it seems convenient in the moment, it's a squirrely existence that lacks integrity and erodes our own self-esteem in the long-run.

(*Special note: Avoid ghosting in business situations. You may need to deal with this person in the future, so always be professional and finish on a good note.)

A big part of this dehumanizing others (digitally dismissing them) is sheer numbers. We're able to access huge numbers of people and profiles, turning the world into a catalog of potential mates—which becomes an unmanageable number. What comes with this "catalog" are unrealistic expectations: we expect perfection—handsome/beautiful, smart, charming, rich or potential to be rich, kind, caring, funny. So, we peruse thousands of "potentials", make snap judgements, and eliminate the "imperfects". The problem is we never accept our imperfections, which would make us more complete, mature prospects to potential mates.

Then we hit age 30, and hit the panic button (regarding marriage).

Digital relational dysfunction comes in many forms: Cyberstalking and harassment is prevalent, websites have flourished that promote extra-marital affairs, and pornography has proliferated on the Internet. Meanwhile, cyber-bullying has become a serious problem for young people (particularly when relationships go bad), in some cases leading to violence and suicides. So, we need to be careful with how deeply we dive into this often opaque world of cyber-mating.

Remember this ancient American proverb: "If it seems too good to be true, it probably is." Or, we might say "Buyer beware" when shopping online for love. Take your time.

Mr. Right?

Anybody can be charming and delightful online. Here's an example;

"He met his future wife, Sitora Yusufiy, on MySpace in 2008. Both were on the site looking for love and eventually marriage, and she was drawn to him because of his alluring and funny messages."

Who was this alluring and funny guy? Omar Mateen, who killed 49 people during an attack at a night club in Orlando, Florida. It was a classic case of rushing into a relationship.

I mentioned earlier some of the frustrations young women have with meeting young men, who have been increasing their gaming while reducing their mating behaviors. But to be fair, "it takes two to tango", and many single men have told me that it's hard to meet and communicate with women who are fixated on their phones. The young men I spoke with told me that they find it difficult to meet women in Taipei because many women are too busy looking at their phones, or talking/texting on their phones, so they're not available for the initial, "break the ice" conversation.

No space for serendipity   Watching dance videos at a wedding

It's impossible to make eye contact and initiate chit-chat when everybody's looking down. Thus, we're unavailable for so many of those serendipitous meetings that change lives. For both men *and* women in Taipei, it's possible that you've missed that "right" person because of constantly looking down.

*Note to guys: if the gal is really into her phone, you'll be sharing her with the phone after marriage, so address it prior to the wedding. I've seen TV shows here in Taiwan where couples have described how their mate spends more time on LINE, Facebook and texting than talking to them, interfering with emotional and intellectual connection. Usually, they won't talk about it—until they have an argument.

Recently, while eating dinner in the food court at the Vie Show Cinemas Hsin Yi, a young couple (both about 25 years old) sat down next to me. They were having some drinks, and "sort of talking". I say sort of talking because for 30 minutes, as the young man spoke, the young lady was looking at her phone, grooming herself, sending LINE messages, taking selfies, and only half-paying attention to her date (who was not looking at his phone).

If I take 50 of these, one of them will be good

An occasional selfie is fine—they can be cute or funny. But a FB wall full of dramatic selfies raises red flags. Actually, it's a cry for love, for attention. That's true whether you're a man or a woman. We all seek acknowledgement, we want approval and connection—but more selfies is not the solution. When I see a FB wall full of selfies I wonder "What is going on with this person?" and "Where's the rest of the person?" A better way to show well-roundedness and attractiveness would be a variety of posts that show activities we enjoy and participate in, organizations we belong to and photos where we look less than perfect—it conveys realism.

Dying to Selfie

Speaking of selfies, be careful—it can be **hazardous** to your health, even deadly. A Japanese tourist died after taking a selfie at the Taj Mahal, in India. And many others have been seriously injured or died while trying to get that "ultra-cool" selfie that will garner likes, envy and admiration on Facebook. Here are two articles on selfie-insanity:

98

<u>A note to parents and adults of all ages:</u>

Maybe we're sending the wrong messages about mating and marriage to children and teens. I see so many marriages that lack joy, happiness, affection, and fun—especially when children enter the picture. Our children and teens see these joyless unions and justifiably wonder "why would I want that?" Too often, marriage drifts into nothing more than an economic equation. We need to set a better example for the next generations, because the examples of marriage that we're giving them now are uninspiring. And we adults set terrible examples for conflict resolution (we avoid it), which is then passed on to our kids. It's no surprise that they might prefer to marry their phone!

<u>Goals and relating</u>

Why do you think joyless marriages and partnerships happen so often?

In Chapter 4 we covered how goal setting will help you to focus your time and energy on activities that help us to achieve things in life, find purpose and bring peace to our daily existence. Here's another very important aspect of goal setting: **goal setting will help you with your relationships.**

(It's amazing: consider how little education we've received on how to communicate and handle relationships—and yet, how many years did we study math? No wonder we're a mess. Men can do calculus, but can't talk to their wives. And we send kids to cram schools for years to get better grades and pass tests, but rarely talk to them about drugs, bullying or teen pregnancy.)

One of the statuses on Facebook for relationships is "It's complicated". Many people use words like "complicated", "confusing" or even "frustrating" to describe the relationships they are in. Having clear goals and life purpose will help you to determine if the person you are with is a good match. This leads to valuable questions like "Does this person have similar goals?"

"Do we have similar purposes?" "Do our characters match well?" Do we have a spiritual connection?

These questions get beyond superficial issues such as he's/she's cute or sexy, he/she has money, the sex is great. Goals force us to dig into deeper issues that lead to more satisfying long-term relationships. If both people have clear goals this will help answer questions that affect relationships—questions like "Should I take a job in a different city?", "Should I go back to school or find another job?" or "Is my partner a match with my life purpose?" Without clear goals, we can be unduly influenced by an incomplete relationship and make poor choices based on temporary factors. And since only 5% of people write down their goals, we can now see how many of the joyless, complicated or even dead relationships came to be that way.

The bigger picture

Young men and women are shying away from marriage for various reasons, with serious consequences for Taiwan. I believe our devices, the Internet and social media contribute to that. This might seem like griping from a technology resistor, and you might say "Times have changed, as has dating and mating." But, consider these four questions in relation to Taiwan;

- **Has the rate of marriage increased or decreased since devices and social media have skyrocketed?**
- **Has the birthrate increased or decreased since devices and social media have skyrocketed?**
- **Are we relationally happier (as a collective) since devices and social media have skyrocketed?**
- **Is gaming and Internet porn contributing to the decline in marriages and birth rate?**

We'll take a look at these issues in the next chapter.

Key Words

Proverb (n)—a saying that expresses a belief or truth

Get a grip (v ph)—to understand something

Delve into (idiom)—to become involved in something, invest time and energy

Intimacy (n)—closeness, kindness, touching, caring

Facet (n)—one part of something

Exploration (n)—searching for something, seeking new information

Motivated (adj)—excited about or interested in reaching a goal

i.e. (abbreviation)—"id est" (Latin), means "that is", such as

Predisposition (n)—a behavior or thought that existed before

Apparent (adj)—clear, easy to understand

Excessive (adj)—too many, too much

Surfing (v)—quickly looking at different websites

Diversion (n)—something that takes your attention away, keeps you busy

Interference (n)—something that gets prevents clear communication or understanding

Stare (v)—to look at something a long time without blinking or moving your eyes

Devote (v)—to spend time and energy on something

Withhold (v)—to keep something from someone, not let them have something

Numb (v)—to have no feeling, to remove emotion

Sensitivities (n)—our ability to feel care for others, to feel sympathy or empathy

Skew (v)—to make something not normal

Perception (n)—how we think about or see things

Avenues (n)—a way of doing something

Pandora's Box (n)—a box that holds many problems and challenges inside

Pitfall (n)—a negative thing, a bad thing or drawback

Misleading (adj)—wrong information that makes people think a certain way

Critical issues (n ph)—important matters

Chance (adj)—not planned, happening by luck

Meat-market (n)—a place for men and women to meet and evaluate others based on appearance

Suitor (n)—someone who wants to impress you

Prospect (n)—someone you are interested in

Flirt (v)—to behave in a way that gets attention, usually for romance

Misrepresentation (n)—not being truthful about something

Monitor (v)—to constantly watch

Smother (v)—to not give any freedom, not let another person have free time

Tethered to (something) (v ph)—connected to something, unable to break free

24/7 (adj)—24 hours a day, seven days a week, all the time, constant

Semi-fictitious (adj)—a half-truth, not the full truth

Recruit (v)—to search for prospects

Leave (n)—some free time during military service

Disguise (v)—to cover up something, to make it look different

Questionable (adj)—not good, doubtful, not having commitment

Character (n)—the aspects of our personality that define who we are

Integrity (n)—be truthful, honest, caring, strong in character

Victim (n)—a person that suffers pain or injury

Lying by omission (v ph)—leaving out information that would be helpful to another person

Evolve (v)—a gradual process of change

Mess with (v ph)—to not treat someone in the right way

Disposable (adj)—easily thrown away

Ghosting (n)—disappearing, not replying to people, not communicating or responding

Technique (n)—a way of doing something, a skill to do a task

Mature (adj)—responsible, wise, kind

Angst (n)—deep frustration, disappointment

Infect (v)—to cause illness, pain

Conflict resolution (n ph)—solving problems between people, talking about disagreements peacefully

Permanent (adj)—stay the same for a long time or forever

Hide and seek (n)—a game in which children hide, and one person tries to find them

Squirrely (adj)—sneaky, lacking integrity, hiding, incomplete

Erode (v)—to wear down, to reduce

Self-esteem (n)—how we feel about ourselves

Dehumanizing (adj)—treating people as less than human, treating them poorly

Access (v)—to see something, to get information

Catalog (n)—a book that shows many products for sale

Potential (adj)—something that might happen, could be good

Unmanageable (adj)—we can't control properly

Unrealistic (adj)—not based in facts, out of touch

Peruse (v)—to look through something

Snap judgement (n ph)—quickly deciding something or somebody is good or bad based on very little information

Imperfect (adj)—not perfect, having flaws

The panic button (n)—a metaphor for experiencing extreme stress and worry about a situation

Dysfunction (n)—not operating properly, odd behavior

Cyberstalking (n)—following somebody digitally, checking on them too much, bothering them

Harassment (n)—saying or doing unkind things to a person

Prevalent (adj)—many places, widespread, very common

Flourished (v)—to succeed, to do well, become popular

Extra-marital affair (n)—having a relationship with someone who is not your wife or husband

Pornography (n)—sexual images and videos

Proliferate (v)—to become widely popular, used everywhere

Cyber-bullying (n)—treating somebody very badly online, threatening them, abusing them

Opaque (adj)—not clear, not easy to understand

Buyer beware (figure of speech)—we cannot be sure what we are buying is a good or bad product

It takes two to tango (cliché)—arguments, disagreements and struggles involve two people

Fixated (adj)—paying too much attention to something

Break the ice (idiom)—speak the first words, give the first greeting

Initiate (v)—to begin something

Groom (v)—to care for our hair, face or body

Half-paying attention (figure of speech)—not giving someone our full attention

Red flag (n)—an indication of trouble

Well-roundedness (n)—indicates good character and personality

Convey (v)—to communicate a message

Send the wrong message (figure of speech)—to give wrong information or examples

Lack (v)—to not have

Affection (n)—showing love toward others, such as hugging, holding hands, kissing

Justifiably (adj)—having reason to think, believe or do something

Uninspiring (adj)—something that doesn't motivate us, doesn't move us to action

Prefer (v)—choosing one thing over another

Aspect (n)—a point, an issue

Complicated (adj)—not clear, not easily understood, challenging

Superficial (adj)—fake, only a good image on the surface

Unduly (adj)—for the wrong reasons, giving value to something that is not valuable

Temporary (adj)—for a short period of time

Shying away (idiom)—avoiding

Various (adj)—different things

Gripe (v)—to complain a lot

Resistor (n)—someone who doesn't want to do something, a person who waits a long time

Hazardous (adj)—dangerous to us

9

The Bigger Picture of Love and Technology

"Health is the greatest gift, contentment the greatest wealth,
faithfulness the best relationship"

Buddha

I finished the previous chapter with these questions;

- **Has the rate of marriage increased or decreased since devices and social media have skyrocketed?**
- **Has the birthrate increased or decreased since devices and social media have skyrocketed?**
- **Are we relationally happier (as a collective) since devices and social media have skyrocketed?**
- **Is gaming and Internet porn contributing to the decline in marriages and birth rate?**

The marriage rate in Taiwan has decreased, (divorce rate stagnant), and the birth rate in Taiwan has decreased—raising dogs is easier;

Only you can answer if you're happier in relationships. As for collective relational happiness, my conversations with people indicate that we are more distant from each other, and experience more discontent. All you have to do is look around and see if people are relating or isolating.

There's no data regarding gaming and Internet porn's impact on marriage and birth rate. What do you think? Do you think gaming and Internet porn are increasing Taiwan's marriage and birth rates? I doubt it.

Certainly, many factors impact marriage and birth rates. Economics plays a big role, as does aging, education and employment. **But have we** turned a blind eye **to technology's role in the declines of Taiwan's marriage and birth rates?**

If you'd like a glimpse **of Taiwan's** demographic **future, all you have to do is look northwest to Japan.** The arc of Japan's and Taiwan's economic and societal development are remarkably similar, with Taiwan's trends lagging a few years behind. The article (QR code below), *NEET Goes Global*, explores how similar the (tech) cultures are, and includes this quote by Taiwan film director Edward Yang—"If you don't want to go out into society, society isn't going to come looking for you."

By 2050, Japan's population will drop by 25%, from 127,000,000 today to 97,000,000. By 2060, Taiwan's population will drop by 22%, from 23,000,000 today to 18,000,000 (and we'll be a much older society as the median age climbs). Japan and Taiwan have remarkably similar birthrates which place them near the bottom of world rankings. To maintain a steady population, countries need a fertility rate of 2.1. In the CIA 2015 World Factbook listing of 224 countries and territories, Taiwan is #221,

Japan is #211; both far below the 2.1 fertility rate for maintaining population. Here's a link to the chart;

Birth and aging factors will have profound impacts on quality of life (who will do the work?), and economies (declining). Both places have rising longevity, increasing the burden on younger generations, along with strict (Japan) and relatively strict (Taiwan) anti-immigration policies which hurt population replenishment. (And Taiwan will not always be able to rely on Philippine, Indonesian and Vietnamese housekeepers to do the dirty work.)

Japan and Taiwan experienced economic miracles (which have crested), that produced higher incomes and greater standards of living. In Japan, one could say the economic miracle produced the perfect society—including all the technology anybody could desire. Japan has everything--**except mating couples!**

How does this affect our future?

If we take a big picture look at Taiwan, we see the same societal arcs.

Younger generations in Japan have lived in technology for 20 years, leading to an over-reliance on games, gadgets and devices for entertainment. The result? Young people don't meet, don't marry, don't mate and don't have babies. There are social programs to counsel legions of men who are in their 30's and 40's who have never been on a date and have no idea how to talk to a woman, as this article explains (link on next page);

Consider this quote from an article in the Nikkei Asian Review;

"The rise of social media is eroding the amount of fact-to-face communication between people. In Japan, one upshot of this phenomenon is that younger people are finding it increasingly difficult to share their problems with those around them. In essence, they feel as though they have no one to turn to for advice."

Here is a recent population chart for Taiwan, showing the number of people by age group. Look at the bottom two age groups;

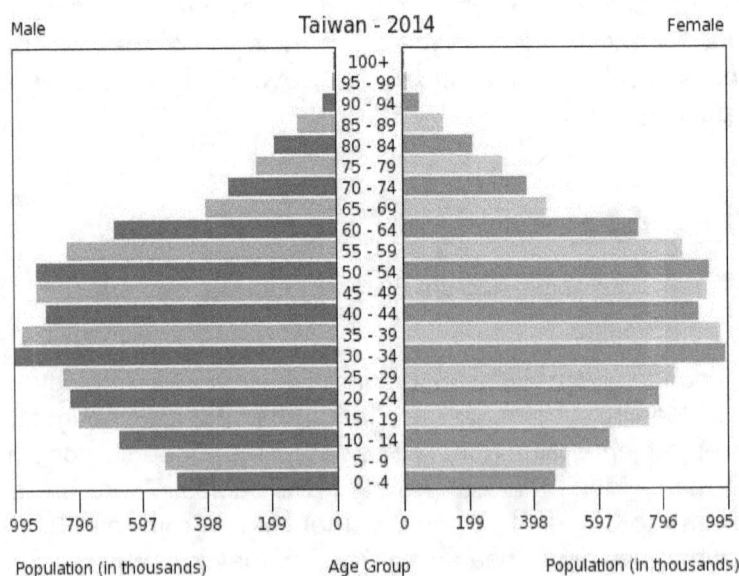

Now, jump forward to 2050. This is our future;

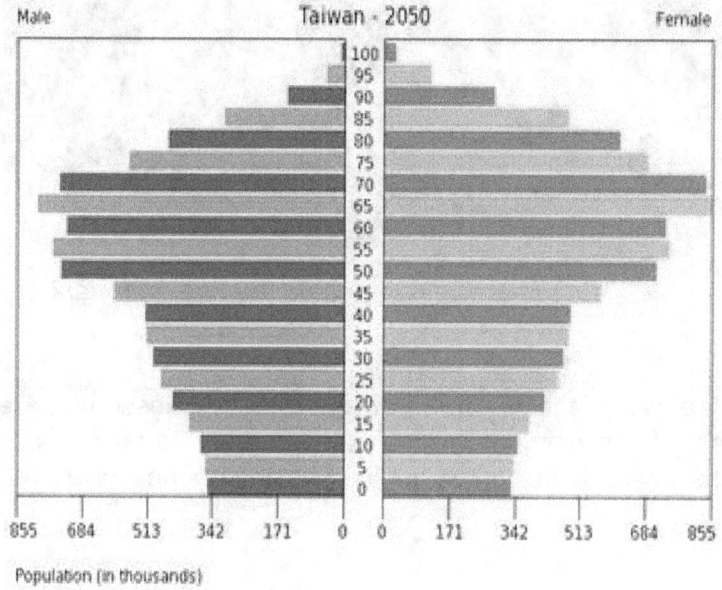

In Taiwan and Japan we might be scrolling, texting and gaming our way to extinction.

It may be too late for Taiwan to turn things around regarding population issues. Like Japan, we have everything—convenient transportation, great healthcare, and entertainment right in the palm of our hand. But it's pretty clear that phones, tablets, the Internet and social networking don't enhance reproductive mating—the form of mating which leads to the type of family building that helped to create the incredibly motivated populace that built Taiwan.

Today, even if families have kids, too often the parents are spending time looking at their devices. Children just want us to be present, look, listen—they want attention. We don't have to do anything except be there, but many times we're distracted—and the kids see us. What example are we setting for them?

Whatever is on the phone must be very important

Are we teaching our children the right lessons? Are we teaching them how to communicate properly, to be considerate toward others, to listen—or are we passing on the isolation model of behavior?

What messages are we sending?—because the kids are watching

Dads watching their phones while moms watch the kids

There are a lot of lonely, sad, frustrated and confused people right around us. We all seek love, attention, and connection—but then we escape into our phones. Are we finding what we desire?

At a recent seminar I led, I had the participants give a presentation at the end. One of the speakers, Henry Chen, a 26 year-old IT professional admitted that before he met his wife, his best friend was his phone. I loved Henry's honesty and bravery; he shared this with 25 people. It was a rare admission—something many people today experience, but few will admit—that their phone is their best friend. By talking about this in a mature way, Henry helped everybody, and communicated truth that is rarely seen or heard. He's a good guy—great personality, hardworking, engaging, and honest about himself, which helps him and others to grow.

Me, with Henry Chen 陳彥衡

Improved moods?

Are we happier with our devices? On a very serious note, has the rate of depression gone down in the past ten years? Has the rate of suicide gone down?

According to the World Health Organization, South Korea is second in national suicide rates, Japan is 17th. Taiwan is not listed in the WHO rankings, but other sources place Taiwan close to Japan. If you go back over the previous ten years, the rates have been about the same for all three. While there are many cultural and societal reasons for national suicide rates, it's clear that the advent of the digital age has not alleviated the problem of suicide. It's possible that it's made things worse by increasing isolation.

Interestingly, while Japan, Korea and Taiwan are considered advanced economies, most of the other top 25 countries around them in suicide rankings would be considered "less-developed"—

many of those countries aren't even close to having the income, infrastructure and lifestyles that exist in Taiwan, Japan and Korea. We have so many good things, but we're still discontent. What's going on? (Here's a link to suicide rankings;)

This is one of those conversations we're not having here in Taiwan. Instead, we sweep it under the rug. In my hometown of Pittsburgh, a local high school has seen an increase in suicides in the past five years. This is alarming to the community, so they're having some forums on this (link below);

Are we having any such dialogue here in Taiwan—not just for students, but for all ages, especially vulnerable 20-40 year-olds?

When it comes to alleviating our emotional ailments it seems that our new idols (the devices) don't work any better than our previous methods of communication. We keep looking for love in all the wrong places; not just romantic love, but connection with people—real, kind love from others and for others—and we're not finding it.

The move away from spoken conversation and active listening has deeply profound consequences for individuals and our society.

Key Words

Turn a blind eye (figure of speech)—to not see something, usually by choice, not admit a problem

Glimpse (n)—a quick look at something

Demographics (n)—information about a group of people in a city or country, such as age, education, sex

Arc (n)—a curve on a graph that represents numbers

Trend (n)—a pattern that has developed

Lag behind (idiom)—to follow something, a delay

Median (n)—the exact middle unit of a group of units

Fertility rate (n)—the number of babies that a woman will give birth to in her child-bearing years

Longevity (n)—how long we can expect to live

Burden (n)—a heavy weight to carry, a difficulty

Strict (adj)—very limited, not flexible

Relatively (adv)—in comparison to something else

Replenishment (n)—the re-supply of something, to add back in

Rely (v)—to expect something to happen or someone to do something

The dirty work (n ph)—work that most people don't want to do

Crest (v)—to reach the highest point, and then start to come back down

Over-reliance (n)—depending too much on something

Counsel (v)—to give advice, listen with care

Legions (n)—many thousands

Extinction (n)—when a species dies off, no more exist

Turn things around (idiom)—make things better, improve the situation

Networking (v)—connecting with people for business or social purposes

Enhance (v)—to make something better

Incredibly (adv)—amazing, great, surprising

Populace (n)—the citizens of a city or country

Considerate (adj)—thinking of others, being kind toward them

Model (n)—an example

Admission (n)—a statement of truth about yourself

Advent (n)—the arrival of something, rising, increasing

Alleviate (v)—to relieve pain, reduce pressure

Infrastructure (n)—facilities and services that countries need, such as hospitals, highways, trains, ports

Sweep it under the rug (figure of speech)—to cover up a bad thing, not admit that it exists

Ailment (n)—a sickness, a feeling of discomfort

Seoul Subway I-cell-ation 2007

Here's a video I took on the Seoul subway nine years ago—long before we started doing this;

10

I'm not bothering anybody

"A human being is a part of the whole called by us universe, a part limited in time and space. He experiences himself, his thoughts and feeling as something separated from the rest, a kind of optical delusion of his consciousness. This delusion is a kind of prison for us, restricting us to our personal desires and to affection for a few persons nearest to us. Our task must be to free ourselves from this prison by widening our circle of compassion to embrace all living creatures and the whole of nature in its beauty."

Albert Einstein

Seldom do we think about how our behavior impacts others. "I'm just doing my thing" we tell ourselves. Einstein thought otherwise;

"This delusion is a kind of prison for us, restricting us to our personal desires and to affection for a few persons nearest to us."

We see that manifested today as we isolate in our digital circles, not acknowledging those who exist outside our network. But as the Albert Einstein quote asserts, we're not separated from everybody; we're all connected, so that requires a humane level of consideration toward others.

One of the most famous bible verses is Luke 6:31: "Do to others as you would have them do to you"

Do we practice that? It's one thing to be kind, gracious and helpful to the people we know, but the real measure of our character is if we are kind, gracious and helpful to people we don't know.

(Note: If you're looking for a mate, watch how they treat strangers.)

Checking out while dining out

Have you noticed in restaurants how phones have become a significant part of the meals? Almost everybody at dining room tables will have a phone next to them. The degree of engagement varies, but we've all seen situations where there is significant phone activity, rather than engagement with the people at the table. Some people bail out of the conversation for long periods of time—sometimes there's little conversation at all—and this while dining with family and friends.

Rather than spending time talking to each other, I often see families spending dinner scrolling Facebook or LINE. It's kind of sad, because this is a time for people to share ideas with each other, to get to know and understand each other better. Instead, we block these openings, and waste these rare opportunities to bond.

We already spend enough time during the day looking at screens; can't we just eat, look at each other and talk?

Dr. Uri Hasson has done some fascinating work into the speaking-listening dynamic. Using MRI images of the brains of speakers and listeners that share stories, Hasson discovered that "neural coupling" occurs, which underlies successful communication. In simpler terms, Hasson has scientific evidence that speaking and listening does bond people together—which is why families should talk rather than text.

Here's a link to an article on Dr. Hasson's findings;

And here's a link to an excellent TED Talk, in which Dr. Hasson explains this neural coupling process, along with brain scan images that illustrate the positive changes in our brains from conversing;

I've also noticed how we (diners) don't acknowledge the waiters and waitresses very much as they tend to our needs. "Thank you" or nods of approval as they bring food or refill our water have been replaced by silence, as we barely notice them while we are looking down. I'm not sure we even taste the food, combining eating and screen time. (Note: A window into a person's character is how they treat waiters and waitresses, especially if a mistake is made.)

Our phone activity at meals adds a good deal of time to the dining process. We take longer to order food since we're "phone busy" before looking at menus. Meals take longer as we alternate between eating, scrolling and photographing our food. And many groups linger a long time after the meals, all busy with phone activity.

Meanwhile, the wait staff literally becomes a "waiting" staff as meals morph into scrolling sessions. In America, waiters and waitresses depend on tips for their income, so the longer meals reduce their income. In Taipei, tips are not the norm, but I must remember that these waiters and waitresses are real people, with a job to do, so it behooves me to finish my meal is a reasonable amount of time, and respect their time.

Just because I'm a paying customer doesn't make me a tenant.

This dining-digital activity not only affects the wait staff, but also the restaurant and waiting customers. Restaurants turn over fewer tables as meals drag on, and customers who are waiting for tables have to wait longer; both of which impact the profit margins for the restaurants. I've watched some people finish their meals, then spend 15 or 20 minutes playing with their phones, while there is a line of people waiting outside.

It's not just fine dining establishments that are affected. Have you ever gone into Mos Burger, McDonald's, or the B1 food court of Taipei 101, ordered your food, and can't find a place to sit? I've seen families walk around with trays of food, scanning for a table, only to find that many tables are occupied by folks that have long finished eating but are busy with phones or tablets. Or try Starbucks on the weekend, when seats are occupied for hours and hours, long after the coffee has been finished. On several occasions I've walked around these places before ordering my food or drinks, scanning for available seats, only to find every table occupied—then I left without buying anything.

In a collective way, this phone activity creates a domino effect, where all customers spend more time on this waiting, eating and drinking activity, creating a cumulative time vacuum.

The Weight room becomes the "Wait room"

The gym I belong to is very crowded, particularly in the evenings and on the weekends. While there are aerobics classes, weight machines and treadmills, it has also become a place for members to give their fingers and thumbs heavy workouts. Almost everybody is walking around with a phone in their hand. Is it really necessary? Can we not exercise for an hour without checking social media, watching videos or making phone calls? When I exercise I usually leave my phone in my locker, because I'm not that important, and if somebody wants to call me, then it can wait until I finish exercising.

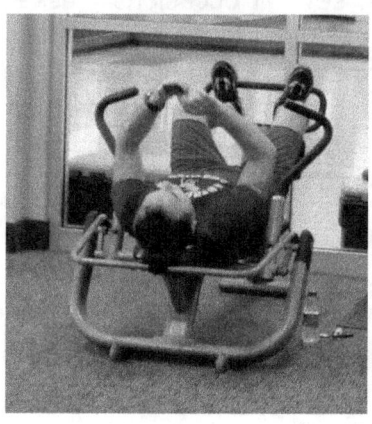

While the phone activity creates additional navigational issues, rerouting around people standing around looking at their phones, the biggest problem is members sitting on equipment; not using the equipment, but spending time on Facebook, LINE, sending text messages, watching videos or making calls. It's not inconsequential: many other members want to use the equipment but have to wait as workout routines have ballooned in time, due to digital distractions, creating a collective time vacuum.

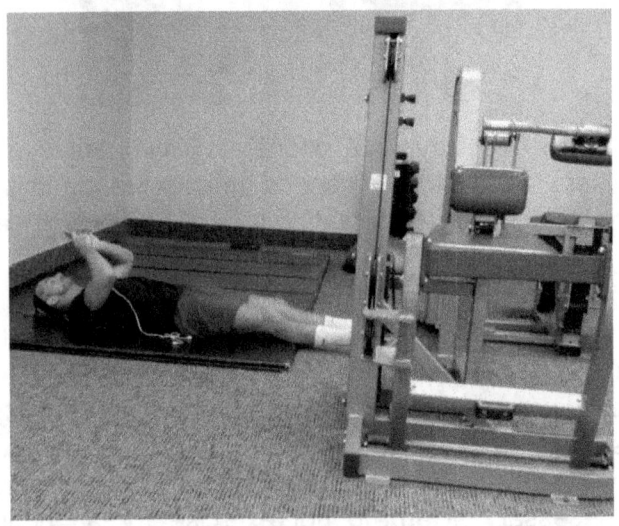

He could have done this at home.

Some gyms have signs posted on the walls that advise members not to use their phones so much in the exercise areas, but nobody reads the signs. On several occasions I asked the staff to intervene, but they were reluctant to do so, just shrugging and saying "What can we do?" On a few occasions I took matters into my own hands and asked people to let me use the equipment and they've gotten angry, almost resulting in fights.

Once, I waited for a machine as the user sat on it, looking at his phone. I timed him: seven minutes he sat there. Nobody else could use it—and then, he got up and walked away. Seven minutes might not seem like much, but this was a piece of equipment that several people wanted to use—so we all waited while he watched his video.

Stalls and desks

Have you ever gone into the toilet and become immersed in your phone? Yes, it happens. It sounds ridiculous, but bathrooms are another area that we make people wait, while we do our phone thing. Does it matter? Just wait until you need to go the bathroom, and someone has the door locked, busy scrolling or texting.

Did you ever make anybody at work wait for your response, or for some task to be done by you? "I'm so busy" is a favorite excuse as to why we delay replies and work, yet there's always time for surfing and social networking. Just look at your Facebook news feed during the day, and it's pretty obvious from the posts, comments and likes that there's plenty of FB activity going on during work hours, resulting in other people waiting for work to be completed. The same is true with LINE, and streams full of stickers all day long—supposedly while everybody is working.

Half the people at this table aren't paying attention to the speaker—a common work scenario

I mentioned in Chapter 7 how multi-tasking makes our roads dangerous. Multi-tasking also affects our productivity at work, at home, while studying, etc. Many studies have shown that we're actually less productive when we multi-task. Here's a quote from a study released by the American Psychological Association (link to the article below quote);

"Psychologists who study what happens to cognition (mental processes) when people try to perform more than one task at a time have found that the mind and brain were not designed for heavy-duty multitasking."

Stanford professor Clifford Nass did some revealing studies on multi-tasking before he passed away. His conclusion? Multi-tasking is a myth. Here's the link;

His summary was that we are less productive when we multi-task. In a TED Talk that he gave, he listed four characteristics of chronic multi-taskers;

- Poor filtering (poor at separating what is important/not important)
- Ineffective memory management (easily forget)
- Suckers for irrelevancy (waste time on unimportant things)
- Bad at multi-tasking! (unproductive)

Here's a link to the video of his TED Talk;

In his TED Talk, Nass shares brain scans that show differences in brain functioning when multi-tasking—it takes up too much RAM in our brain, like a computer trying to run too many programs. And now bunches of us are making others wait as we multi-task.

A bad place to multi-task—unaware the light turned green (this happens often at intersections)

Phones and tablets aren't going away, nor should they. Yes, we have busy, stressful lives, so we may not have a sense of urgency when we're relaxing at a restaurant or exercising at the gym. But we need to be conscientious toward others—not just our family and friends, not just the small network of people that we know, but to all those strangers out there: strangers who are busy, stressed people just like us, waiting to do what they need to do.

Helpful tips

- At dinner, keep the device usage to a minimum. Talk with your family and friends.
- At the gym, leave the phone in the locker. The cyber world will still be there when you're done.
- At work, set certain times in your schedule when you will check social media. This will help you avoid the constant checking which gobbles up time, interrupts work flow and kills productivity.
- In your car (yes, again, because it is so prevalent)—decide before you drive that you will not text or talk while driving. You must make this decision before you drive, because if you don't, you probably will use your phone. Remember— your vehicle can kill people in a split-second. Obviously, it ruins the victim's life, but it will ruin yours, too. Driving is the worst time to multi-task.

Imagine a distracted driver at this intersection

Key words

Otherwise (adj)—something different

Delusion (n)—a belief that is misleading

Manifest (v)—to come to be, to show the result of an action

Assert (v)—to state something such as an idea or belief

Humane (adj)—treating people and things with respect

Degree (n)—an amount, a measure

Bail out of (something) (idiom)—to stop doing something, to remove yourself

Bond (v)—to grow closer together

Fascinating (adj)—very interesting, amazing

Dynamic (n)—how two or more things interact, a process

MRI (Magnetic Resonance Imaging) (n)—a scan of body parts that shows images for medical purposes

Neural coupling (n)—brain activity in which two or more people have similar reactions

Underlie (v)—to be a base or foundation

Illustrate (v)—to show what something is or how it works

Converse (v)—to have a conversation

Tend to (v)—to lead to an action

Nod (v)—to move your head forward slightly

Alternate (v)—to switch between two or more things

Linger (v)—to spend a long time doing something

Literally (adv)—to lead to something

Morph (v)—to change from one thing into something different

The norm (n ph)—what is normal

Behoove (v)—to do something that is needed or necessary

Tenant (n)—a person that pays rent to live somewhere

Turn over (idiom)—having several different people or groups use something

Drag on (idiom)—taking too long

Margin (n)—the difference between revenue and expenses

Occupy (v)—to be in a place for some period of time

Domino effect (n ph)—how one action affects the next action and following actions

Cumulative (adj)—the total amount of things added up

Vacuum (n)—a device that sucks things up

Aerobics (n)—a form of exercise class that builds endurance and energy

Treadmill (n)—an exercise machine that people walk or run on

Workout (n)—an exercise routine

Reroute (v)—to change directions

Inconsequential (adj)—not important

Balloon (v)—to grow much larger than expected

Intervene (v)—to take action on the part of another

Reluctant (adj)—not wanting to do something, hesitant

Take matters into (one's) own hands (figure of speech)—to do something yourself when others won't

Immerse (v)—to become completely involved in something

Obvious (adj)—very clear to see or know

Supposedly (adv)—something that should be

Productivity (n)—the amount of work that is done or things made

Revealing (adj)—showing information that tells much about something we may not know

Pass away (v)—to die

Myth (n)—a story that may not be true

Chronic (adj)—doing something again and again, repeatedly

RAM (Random Access Memory) (n)—the memory on your computer that runs programs

Bunch (n)—a group

Conscientious (adj)—caring about others, being kind

Sense of urgency (n ph)—an interest in getting things done now, knowing something is important

Gobble up (idiom)—to use up a lot of something

11

We're not connecting the dots

"There are many things of which a wise man might wish to be ignorant"

Ralph Waldo Emerson

I've noticed that folks can get pretty defensive about their digital habits. Some people will strongly disagree with some points I make; others will agree with the issues raised. Either way, that's okay—I realize that our digital habits have become a deeply personal issue and choice. My goal is to get people to think about this digital addiction that is wrapping its hands around us, how it affects our behaviors and relationships, and how we impact others.

Phones, tablets, social media and the Internet are great tools if used judiciously. Ideally, they provide valuable information, help us connect with others, and enable us to execute tasks more efficiently and effectively. That's the ideal. The paradox is that we are inundated with too much information, disconnected from the real humans around us, bogged down by choice and tethered to gadgets that harness us in 24/7 accessibility.

Love, Money, Time, Health

I teach many classes and seminars to children, teens and adults, and in one activity I ask "What's most important; Love, Money, Time or Health?"

What do you think?

There's always a healthy discussion, and there is no absolute right answer—it depends on each person's perspective, age and station in life. But ultimately the debates lead to health and time as most valuable. Without good health, life can be constantly challenging. Without time, well, we have no life. **Ironically, in our daily lives we think most about money and love, take for granted our health, and rarely consider that our time on Earth is finite.**

On a daily basis, what can you control the most?

Your time, and how you use it.

We're all given 1,440 minutes in a day: some people use them wisely, others not so. Our phones and tablets, the Internet and social media can save us tons of time if used wisely. But these tools and platforms also squander time if we are not good stewards. Most of us are not connecting the dots as to how the digital deluge not only gobbles our time, but also affects our emotions, attitude, energy, sleep and relationships on a daily basis. Especially our kids;

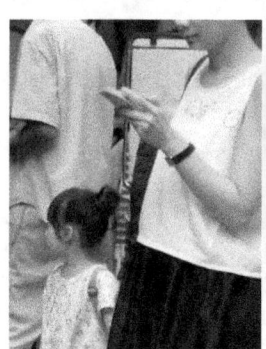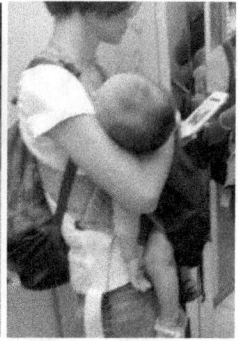

In this and the next few chapters I'll look at the five pillars of our digital behavior; The Internet, Social Media, Facebook, Phones, and Games. As we look into these, consider if they have brought you more peace and lower stress—or less peace and higher stress.

The Internet

With our devices we now have a universe of information available for immediate access. That's great if we are focused and targeted in what we seek (remember Box 2?). But we can also waste immense amounts of time on the Internet if we are not disciplined. Frankly, most of us are not disciplined. I've wasted much time reading articles, watching videos and chasing links that had nothing to do with accomplishing my goals in life. A little temporary entertainment is okay, but most of us wander into the digital forest and can't find our way out.

The quote at the beginning of this chapter, *"There are many things of which a wise man might wish to be ignorant"* underlines our need not to know everything. TMI—too much information, can be debilitating. Studies have been done that show today's managers experience decision fatigue and higher stress due to TMI. So, do we need to know everything? The Internet is full of information—our problem is filtering it, and the time and mental energy that takes. Here's an article from the Harvard Business Review titled "Why Wise Leaders Don't Know Too Much";

Have you ever applied critical thinking to your Internet activity, time and mental energy?

In the newspaper business, the saying used to be "Bad news sells", which explains why certain stories would be on the front page. Then TV news modified this to "If it bleeds, it leads", which is why the first story you see is some disaster or violent act. Since newspapers and TV news are now passé, this editorial strategy has leaped to our backlit screens, assaulting our senses from endless sources.

While the Internet is a great source of news and information, it's also an ocean of frivolous news and misinformation, and most of us don't understand why it operates the way it does. It's hundreds of thousands, possibly millions of websites fighting for your attention, doing everything they can to get your clicks. That's why headlines, stories, photos and videos are posted in the most provocative ways, designed to generate emotions within you to get you to click on them. So then we wade in, deeper and deeper, spending our valuable time sifting through pulp. More clicks, more time on sites and more visits to those sites all equal more advertising revenue for the websites—and the weirder, more extreme the story is, the more clicks it gets.

One of the pioneers in the development of the Internet, Leonard Kleinrock, offered these thoughts in a paper he wrote back in 2004;

"A system that is founded to include any and all information — contributed by anyone who chooses to contribute — will naturally include some pretty terrible stuff." And, he adds, *"Gone are the days when we could trust what came to us through the net, when we could expect that what was directed at us was relevant, useful, accurate and benign,"* he wrote. *"Now we find ourselves confronted with junk, attacked by viruses, denied access, worried about our privacy, and confused about who can provide relief to these and other concerns."*

Here's the link;

We need to contemplate what the constant stream of negative news does not only to our individual psyche, but also the collective psyche of our society. In America, I think it's contributed to a greater level of anger. In Taiwan, has more information and the constant flow of gossip and negative news improved our daily lives?

Then there's YouTube, which can be a great learning and entertainment platform, yet perversely attracts millions of views for videos of people getting hurt, maimed or killed. Yes, sadly, there are videos that have garnered millions of views that show humans being killed. I fear that we're becoming numb to such things.

The Internet's twist on "If it bleeds, it leads" is to present juxtapositions of the sublime and the ridiculous. First you'll see a posting about ISIS beheading twenty people, and the next story will be about a celebrity having an affair. Does that absurdity ever register with us? Then photos of an explosion in India that kills 50 people, followed by "Ten ways to get a flat stomach", with constant teasers flashing by in a matter of seconds with a goal of getting you hooked.

What information is so important that we don't look when we are moving, even on stairs?

And don't care where we stop—right in the middle--forcing others to move around us.

Did you ever notice how there's so much celebrity news on the Internet?

Most celebrities, politicians, even top corporate execs have social media managers all striving for your attention (i.e. your time). The social media managers create "exposure" plans, such as six-weeks of strategically timed and placed updates on the celebrity. In most instances, the social media manager is making the post, not the celebrity. So, much of the celebrity news you are bombarded with is part of contrived plans to keep the celebrities in the news. It sells CDs, movie and concert tickets, gets votes and keeps the masses talking about people that really don't matter in our lives.

Political news is manipulated to create the most controversy (e.g. Donald Trump, Ko Pe). And sports news has gone off the deep end, focusing more on rumors and negative personal stories than games and scores, instigating conflict and arguments because our attention is drawn to drama.

Finally, the Internet has given us "Victim du jour", that unfortunate person who made a mistake or said/done something stupid. Their story or video goes viral, and then they are crucified online. The cyber-universe sets about online shaming without knowing the person or the context of what they said or did. The cyber-universe can be like a pack of wild dogs that has sniffed blood, revealing a dark side of our society—much of which comes through in comment sections beneath articles, which should be retitled "Complain, Insult and Argue" sections. These comments are frequently full of profanities and gross statements (often posted by anonymous trollers).

Here's a link to a revealing TED Talk about a woman whose life was ruined via online shaming due to a (misinterpreted) tweet she posted;

There is much anger circulating on the Internet.

We can do better.

A bit more substance

For regional news and analysis, I suggest the Nikkei Asian Review. And blogs can be a good source of some deeper communication and critical thinking. The problem is that in today's "microwave society" we have little patience for extended reading. One blogger that I do check out every now and then is James Altucher. He has some excellent insights into many of the challenges of everyday life. Here's a link to his blog;

Key Words

Defensive (adj)—protecting one's position, actions, behaviors or ideas

Judiciously (adv)—using good judgement

Ideally (adv)—the best option, choice or situation

Enable (v)—to allow or help us to do something

Paradox (n)—two things that are connected to each other but totally opposite

Disconnected (adj)—not connected, apart

Bogged down (idiom)—stuck in something, not making progress

Harness (v)—to control or restrain something

Accessibility (n)—available, easy to see, hear or know

Absolute (adj)—the one correct possibility

Perspective (n)—how a person sees or thinks about things

Ultimately (adv)—in the end, the final outcome

Finite (adj)—limited

Squander (v)—to waste something

Steward (n)—a person who is given responsibility over something

Connect the dots (v ph)—to bring together facts that solve a problem or mystery

Pillar (n)—a support, something that holds weight up

Immense (adj)—very large

Frankly (adv)—candid, honest

Wander (v)—to move about in no particular direction

Debilitating (adj)—weakening, hampers our efforts

Fatigue (n)— a feeling of being very tired, exhausted

Filter (v)—to separate things, to choose we want to keep

Modify (v)—to change, improve

Passé (adj)—not in fashion any more, not popular

Editorial (adj)—the style of journalism chosen

Assault (v)—to hurt or harm someone or something

Frivolous (adj)—silly, unimportant

Click (n)—the action of choosing a website or other online option

Provocative (adj)—designed to get a response, to anger or excite

Wade in (idiom)—slowly move into an unknown area

Sifting through (something) (idiom)—looking at many things to find one thing

Pulp (n)—material or information that is of low quality

Perversely (adv)—things done in a weird, sometimes offensive way

Twist (n)—a way of doing or making things

Juxtaposition (n)—two things that seem opposite that are put together

Sublime (adj)—serious, logical

Ridiculous (adj)—silly, stupid

Absurdity (n)—something that is very strange, odd

Register with (idiom)—to understand the full meaning of something

Teaser (n)—a small thing designed to get your attention

Flashing (v)—appearing for a very short period of time

Hooked (adj)—attracted to something, persuaded to like or use something

Exposure (n)—publicity, promotion of a person or thing to get attention

Contrived (adj)—doesn't happen naturally

The masses (n)—large groups of people

Manipulate (v)—to control somebody or something in tricky ways

Controversy (n)—something that causes people to get upset or argue

e.g. (abbreviation)—"exempli gratia" (Latin), means example given, for example

Go off the deep end (figure of speech)—losing control, losing our mind

Instigate (v)—to get something started like a fight or argument

Du jour (n)—"of the day" (French)

Viral (adj)—something that becomes very popular very quickly on the Internet

Crucified (v)—to be punished in a severe way

Shaming (n)—saying or doing bad things to embarrass a person

Context (n)—the complete meaning of something, the entire story

Sniff (v)—to smell something to see what it is

Retitle (v)—to change the title

Insult (n)—a negative comment about somebody

Profanities (n)—very bad language

Gross (adj)—disgusting, very unpleasant

Anonymous (adj)—the identity of the person is hidden

Troller (n)—a person that makes negative comments online

Misinterpret (v)—to misunderstand, not get the real meaning

Tweet (n)—140 character statements on Twitter

Circulating (v)—going around, being seen or heard by many people

Microwave society (n ph)—a culture that expects everything to happen fast

Notice the posture; neck, shoulders. I'll talk about this in Chapter 15.

12

Time Vacuums

"No matter how busy you are, you must take time to make the other person feel important"

Mary Kay Ash

Social Media

In Chapter 2 I mentioned that many students answer "I don't know" when I ask them why they're constantly looking at their phones. Often the driver of this activity is FOMO—Fear of Missing Out. Our fear of missing out has been elevated to schizophrenic levels, and it's not just high school or university students that suffer this malady—plenty of adults now have FOMO. FOMO leads to pathological checking, scrolling, rechecking and re-scrolling of LINE, Facebook, Twitter, texts, etc.

I wish there was an app that measured how much time we spend in these activities—it might add up to several hours each day; hours that could be spent learning a new skill or language, working on a meaningful project, helping others or simply cleaning up our own lives.

The opposite of FOMO is our compulsion to share every detail of our life. Where we eat, the park we're visiting, the movie we're seeing—every move we make, every step we take. We used to miss each other and then catch up later, but now we have daily updates on the minutia of life.

We can't even go on vacation now and let it go; we feel the need to post photos and updates several times a day from our exotic destinations, instead of just enjoying the journey and talking about it when we got back home. Ironically, a vacation would be a great time to take a break from social media: it's the perfect opportunity to forget about all the people and things back home, and immerse yourself in the moment.

In North America and Europe Twitter usage has exploded. This platform that allows 140 characters to convey information instantly is sometimes an awesome source of information that can be zapped around the world. Its effective usage has been shown during disasters, political movements and even sporting events, as key information is quickly shared with millions of people. But most of the time Twitter is a string of unimportant statements or opinions, mostly by celebrities or celebrity wannabes with social media agendas. (FYI, singers Katy Perry and Justin Bieber have more Twitter followers than Barack Obama. Apparently, whatever Perry and Bieber are tweeting is more important than the President.) Twitter also has "programmed" posts—posters can pre-arrange posts to appear throughout the day to keep their name popping up, resulting in a constant flow of attention chasing.

LINE is the go-to platform here in Taiwan, and the jury is still out on whether this is a blessing or a curse. Its hypnotic draw explains a large portion of the HD behavior, allowing subscribers to participate in five, ten or more group conversations simultaneously. When I come across a stagger, stop or stall HD'er, usually they're reading, scrolling or responding on LINE.

And when not engaged in LINE, the phone will light up or make a sound to notify you of a new message, resulting in a constant supply of sensory distractions. Much like Pavlov's dogs, we instinctively look again, and again. And again. Yes, you can put the settings on mute, but those conversations still go on, and we check them.

This week, measure the time you spend each day on LINE, and then do a cost/benefit analysis regarding time.

Facebook

Millions of users concurrently digitally beckoning "LOOK AT THIS!" An entire book could be written on Facebook's pros and cons. It's like a marriage that ends in divorce after ten years; there's enough good stuff to hang around that long, but enough bad stuff to drive somebody away. One of the drags that clutters up Facebook (and YouTube, Twitter and other platforms) is what I call "The Attention Chase", where people try to emulate Paris Hilton's recipe of "famous for being famous". It involves constant posting, pleas for likes, and requests that you subscribe to their page or channel.

I didn't really want to join Facebook seven years ago, but it was the only way I could make comments on our company's FB page, allowing me to interact with students and teachers, so I signed up. 900 Friends later I can say it's been a love-hate relationship, wrestling with **the pros and cons of my life being everybody's business**, and vice versa. In the interest of succinctness, here are some bullet points;

- There are winners and losers on Facebook. The winners use it to promote themselves, their companies, their products or services. These people are not interested in you per se, but just your attention, as it often translates into money or them reaching a goal. They're not on Facebook to socialize—it's a one-way street. The "losers" (most of us) are not losers in life, but rather losers of time, money and privacy.

- There is a significant emotional cost in using Facebook excessively. Studies have shown that Facebook actually increases depression. (see below)
- It is a phenomenal distraction that robs time and prevents meaningful progress in areas of our lives that matter in the long-run (it steals time from box 2).
- Facebook is a minimalist way to maintain acquaintances, which scatters our attention and erodes our ability to focus on and develop deep, meaningful relationships.

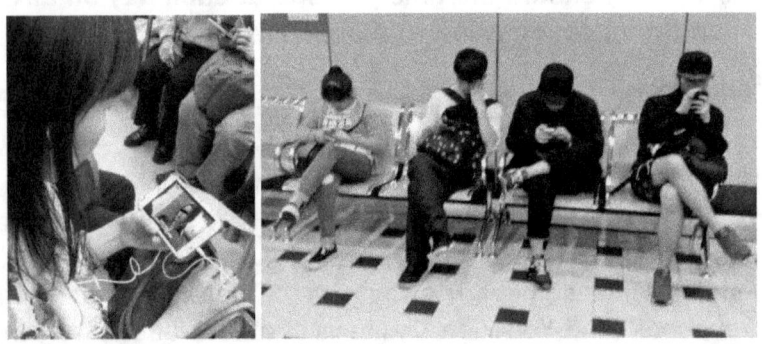

Accumulating a mass of acquaintances doesn't alleviate our loneliness, as Dr. John T. Cacioppo, Director of the University of Chicago Center for Cognitive and Social Neuroscience says in his TEDx Talk *The Lethality of Loneliness*;

"Understanding that it's not the quantity of friends; it's the quality of a few relationships that actually matter." Here's a link to his talk;

In his talk, Dr. Cacioppo highlights the hidden dangers of loneliness, particularly dangers to our physical health. It's an excellent video if you want to understand the impact of isolation.

I'm sorry to spoil your Facebook fun, but if I have, then maybe I've done you a huge favor. Being a spoil-sport is not my intention; getting you to step back and think critically about your quantity of Facebook involvement is. I had to ask myself **"Am I using Facebook to alleviate my loneliness, or does Facebook exacerbate my loneliness?"** Several studies have reported that Facebook actually increases depression. Here's a link to one of them;

Here's a direct link to the University of Michigan study cited in that article;

I've extracted a small section from the Abstract that introduces the University of Michigan study:

"On the surface, Facebook provides an invaluable resource for fulfilling the basic human need for social connection. Rather than enhancing well-being, however, these findings suggest that Facebook may undermine it."

As I read the NPR article I considered the question "What comes first—Facebook, or depression?" I've noticed that my Internet, Facebook and social media activity increases when I am depressed—in some ways it's my escape. The problem is that I've found it to be a downward spiral, with each feeding off the other.

I don't think we've **figured out** this Facebook thing, yet. It takes a while to sort out what purpose it serves in our life; many of us never figure this out—we just spend time on it. In the past year several of my former colleagues at ORTV told me the same thing: that they've cut back their Facebook usage a lot. The message from them is that they find it **redundant**, somewhat "competitive", and after several years of this, an experience of **diminishing returns**. They've asked themselves the questions "What is this?", "Why am I doing this?", and "Is this the best use of my time?"

You may want to ask yourself the same questions.

My life is a password

Digital communication demands can overwhelm us. I have;

- Six email accounts
- Three Facebook accounts
- LINE and WeChat
- One account each for YouTube, LinkedIn, Skype and
    Google+
- Four Dropbox accounts
- Online accounts for my bank, credit card and stock broker
- Several websites that I'm registered for

That's over 25 online accounts, which is a lot of passwords to remember. I didn't have all of this 15 years ago. I could spend all day on these, which is why I'm hesitant to add anything else.

Key Words

Elevate (v)—to raise up to a higher level

Schizophrenic (adj)—unpredictable or extreme ranges of behavior

Malady (n)—an illness

Pathological (adj)—a mentally disturbed condition

Clean up (idiom)—to bring order to something

Compulsion (n)—an unhealthy need to do or have something

Minutia (n)—tiny things that are not important

Zap (v)—to electronically move something very quickly

Wannabe (n)—a person who wants to be important and recognized

FYI (acronym)—"for your information", something I want you to know

The go-to (something) (figure of speech)—the popular or favorite option

The jury is still out (cliché)—a decision has not been made yet

A blessing or a curse (figure of speech)—something that could be good or bad for us

Draw (n)—something that is attractive

Subscriber (n)—a person who signs up for something, agrees to join

Simultaneously (adv)—at the same time

Pavlov's dogs (n ph)—dogs that behaved the same way when hearing a bell, to always react the same way

Instinctively (adv)—to do something without thinking

Cost/benefit analysis (n ph)—an evaluation to determine if something is worth doing

Concurrently (adj)—occurring at the same time

Beckon (v)—to call someone, to get their attention

Pros and cons (n ph)—the good things and the bad things

Divorce (n)—the end of a marriage by legal means

Hang around (idiom)—to spend time waiting somewhere

Drag (n)—a negative thing

Clutter up (v ph)—to make a mess, crowded, disorganized

Emulate (v)—to admire someone to the point of trying to be like them

Wrestle with (idiom)—to struggle with making a decision

Vice versa (adv)—one thing and something that is opposite or different

Succinctness (n)—a short explanation of things, being brief

Bullet point (n)—a short summary of an important point

Per se (adv)—by itself, for one thing

Translate (v)—to turn into something else

One-way street (n ph)—a relationship or communication that only goes in one direction

Phenomenal (adj)—amazing, fantastic, super

Rob (v)—to steal

Minimalist (adj)—the least amount of something, a small effort

Accumulate (v)—to gather many things

Neuroscience (n)—the study of the nervous system

Lethality (n)—something that is deadly

Spoil (v)—to ruin

Spoil-sport (n)—a person who ruins things

Intention (n)—something you want or hope to do

Step back (idiom)—to take a break and think

Exacerbate (v)—to make something worse

Extract (v)—to pull out something

Abstract (n)—a summary of a longer report or study

Undermine (v)—to weaken something

Escape (n)—something that helps us avoid things

Downward spiral (n ph)—bad things that lead to more bad things with no improvement likely

Feeding off (idiom)—when two things contribute to each other

Figure out (idiom)—to understand, to solve a problem

Redundant (adj)—something that keeps repeating the same thing

Diminishing returns (n ph)—less benefit the longer something is experienced, done or used

13

Phones, Games and a Draggin' Boat

"When I let go of what I am, I become what I might be"

Lao Tzu

Phones

Mobile phones, especially smartphones have altered our physical behavior in ways we may not realize. As Sherry Turkle discusses in much of her research, they're "Always on, always on us". We've slid into a reliance of always having our phone with us. When we're moving it's often in our hand—in some ways it's become part of our hand—leading to the auto-reflex of looking at it when it beckons.

Even when the phone isn't beckoning us, our need for distraction during moments of silence or stillness triggers the upward motion followed by looking, checking the various platforms it possesses dozens, sometimes hundreds of times a day.

Think of the dinner digital activity I mentioned in Chapter 10. The moment there's silence or a lull in the conversation, we look at our phone—instead of being in the silence, gathering our thoughts or digesting what was said, and letting the conversation flow to the next point.

At a loss for words

Have phones and social media affected our vocabulary and grammar? Several studies have shown that vocabulary mastery decreases with more texting and social media commenting (which tend to be shorter, relying more on slang, codes, emoticons and stickers.) That's fine for casual communications, but we may be

154

decreasing our vocabulary, which decreases our ability to accurately communicate in more **complex** conversations, written exchanges and negotiations.

At the zoo. Animals are boring?

One thing I need to do on a regular basis is take time to think. Riding my bike, going for walks in the park or exercising at the gym provide opportunities to think about the issues I'm dealing with in my life. They may be work issues, problems in relationships, plans for the present and future, or reflections on past events and lessons learned. This thinking time allows me to connect the dots in my life and formulate appropriate plans and actions.

One of the most important things thinking time allows me to do is figure out how to communicate with the people in my life. Rather than automatically, instantly reacting in many situations, I need time to think or even pray about things. This usually leads to better choices and words on my part, and thus more understanding and better relationships. **If I'm constantly** armed with **my phone and always busy interacting with it, then I** deprive **myself of valuable contemplation time.** Here's an example;

Recently I met with a 26-year-old guy who wanted me to help him prepare for the GMAT, so he could apply to universities in America, in order to pursue an MBA. We met for an hour-and-a-half, and I was confused about how I might help him, and exactly what he needed from me. So, during our meeting, instead of focusing on the GMAT, I "interviewed" him, to find out his history and what his goals were.

After this meeting, I was still confused as to what I could do and what I should tell him. Over the next 24 hours I was able to formulate some ideas for him; ideas that may change the course of his life. It turns out that nobody had ever interviewed him as I did, or given him such feedback. I don't know what he ultimately will do, but I was able to give him some helpful advice.

The only way I was able to organize my thoughts on this matter was by taking time to think about all that he had said. If I had spent too much time on my phone, the Internet or Facebook, I would have been distracted and probably not have come up with a decent game plan for him—and that would have deprived him of the constructive feedback that he needed at this critical juncture in his life.

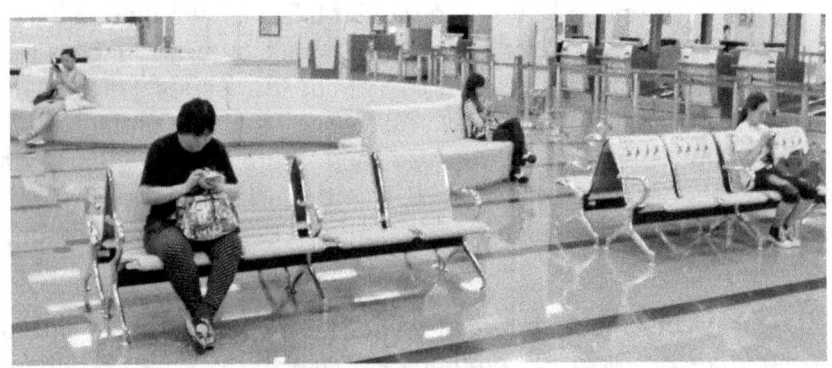

Islands at the airport

How do you break free from the phone?

One of the habits I've developed is purposely leaving my phone at home if I go out for a walk or bike ride. This intentional leaving-behind of the phone now seems unnatural for many of us. But I challenge you to do this once in a while: leave the phone at home, or on your desk at work for brief periods of time while you go and do something.

156

Many of us might feel naked without our phone, but humans survived for thousands of years without phones in their hands. Just go out and enjoy the silence—you might like it. Look at people, say hello, notice the environment around you, observe the flowers in the park, or just be available for serendipitous experiences. Candy Crush can wait. The Korean soap opera can wait. LINE, Facebook, texting and email can wait a few minutes while you absorb life phone-free.

Never free from the phone

This "always on, always on us" phenomenon has led to the expectation of us being instantly accessible. Others now expect it of us, and we expect it of others, which tends to ratchet up our stress levels. This new level of expectations has created demands for explanations—"I sent you a message", "I called your phone three times", "I noticed that you saw my Facebook message an hour ago", "Why was your phone turned off?" Thanks to our phones, **we now have to explain why we didn't respond as quickly as the other person expected!**

Even when relaxing in the park we find it hard to not scroll

Computers were supposed to be the great emancipators of workers, enabling them to complete their tasks more quickly and giving them more free time. Of course, the workplace adjusted and simply added more work for everybody. Our phones and tablets are an extension of this, now enabling us to do work anywhere, anytime, including evenings at home, commutes on buses, or even on airplanes. There's no excuse now for people not to work! It's up to you to set the boundaries; if not, others will do it for you.

At 7 pm on a Wednesday evening recently I was having dinner with my girlfriend Brenda, her daughter Mary and Mary's 3-year-old daughter, Anna. Mary is the Taiwan manager over six retail stores, her regional boss is in Hong Kong, and the headquarters is in Paris. Mary had just arrived home from work at 7:00 pm. Then the Hong Kong boss called Mary's phone at 7:15 and informed her that they were going to have a conference call right then, involving Taiwan, Hong Kong, Paris and a few other locations. Mary had to leave the dinner and retreat to a back room, where she spent the next 90 minutes on this conference call.

This wasn't the first time, and probably won't be the last. At the end of the conference call, nearing 9 pm, Mary staggered out of the back room, mentally drained and frustrated.

We're not realizing what we're doing to people with our expectations of their constant availability.

I've read that the current mayor of Taipei is notorious for his LINE activity, sending messages at all hours, essentially micro-managing issues and employees. One of the problems his administration has had is constant turnover of key staff members. While there are many reasons for these departures, I'm guessing that the non-stop LINE messages don't enhance employee morale. (The same may be true in your workplace.)

But he's not the only executive in Taiwan that does this. I tutor many business people in Taipei, and have heard stories of how corporate usage of LINE has invaded people's lives. We even take our work with us when we go on vacation, rationalizing how invasive it is. One of the attendees at a government seminar I was leading, Leo, shared with me that his week-long vacation to

Taitung was "ruined" because his boss kept sending LINE messages to him, expecting responses. Even on vacation, he was unable to get away from work or his boss.

However, it's not all bad about phones;

One extremely valuable aspect of smartphones and tablets is the lifeline they provide for migrant workers here in Taiwan. We have several Philippine workers at my church and their phones are the only link with their families back home. For them the devices let them maintain connectivity, especially via Skype phone and video calls. Many of them are mothers who work in factories and homes, working brutal schedules, earning sub-par pay while their children are hundreds of miles away. For them, the phones are a blessing.

Games

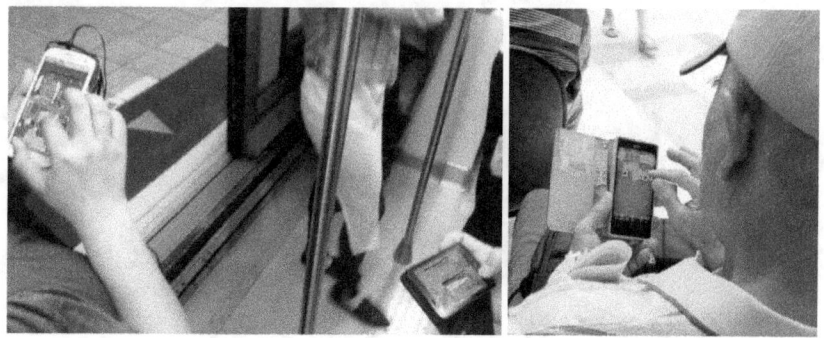

Some people do this all day, then complain about not having enough money or time

I don't play games on my phone (or my laptop at home)—no time for it. I'd rather have a conversation with Brenda or Mary, or spend an hour playing with Anna. Kids see us when we pay more attention to our phones and tablets than to them. The kids just want our time and attention—it's how we show love.

*What item on the phone is more important than our children?
The woman (above) with the stroller is on a street where cars and
motorcycles go crazy fast, and the little boy (below) next to the
street is right where many cars make U-turns, and vehicles often
speed. Notice that the light is green; a mistake could happen in a
few seconds. (One of the moms was gaming)*

A note about games and privacy: many platforms that we sign
up for today require access to all sorts of our information. We're
giving away our privacy. Many sites (not just games) want access
to most of your information. Just recently I read this article about
Pokémon GO wanting access to your email—not just your

contacts, but all your email. They've made a correction, but it's an example of information we can give away without understanding;

Speaking of Pokémon GO, it seems that gaming is taking over our senses, putting playing ahead of consideration toward others or our own safety. We're walking off cliffs and trespassing on others in pursuit of our games. Here's a story about two guys falling off a cliff while playing;

Pokémon GO is neither good nor bad—it just is. It happens to be very popular right now. Sure there are some glitches, like people walking off cliffs or in front of moving cars, but some might consider that Darwinian selection. Just like Angry Birds or Candy Crush, there will always be a new, hot game. Gaming in moderation is fine; the problem is when it becomes a chronic distraction from life purpose, goal achievement and relating.

Connecting the dots

On a micro level, we all need to pause and connect the dots of the Internet, Social Media, Phones and tablets: they're not going away (nor should they). We need to be the masters of them, not they of us.

Are we able to employ moderation? Have we ever tried? Each one of us can do a cost/benefit analysis to determine how digital activity impacts our life. Is the overall effect negative or positive?

How does it affect our families, friends and strangers? How does it affect me and my relationships?

Have these pillars of our digital existence brought us more peace and lowered our stress? Or have we become numb and unaware of the gradually rising digital demands that have crept into our lives and stolen the most valuable thing we have—time?

On a macro level, how is this affecting Taiwan? Are we getting better, staying the same, or falling behind? (FYI, "staying the same" actually means falling behind others who are improving.) Taiwan is a small island with limited resources, and a population that is aging and will soon be shrinking. People are our number one resource. To remain competitive on the global stage we all need to be pulling in the same direction, applying all of the skills and talents we have. Our time and energy is limited and must be channeled in constructive ways. If ¼ or ½ of us are distracted a good bit of the time each day, can Taiwan reach its collective goals?

Imagine this dragon boat—how do you think they'll do in the regional economic race? Will this boat be able to compete with Korea, Japan and Singapore? Will it compete well with the rising economies of Vietnam and the Philippines?

Key Words

Draggin' (slang for dragging) (adj)—not going very fast

Slide into (idiom)—doing something without really thinking about it

Reliance (n)—having to rely on something, needing something to function

Auto-reflex (n)—a physical action we do without thinking

Gather our thoughts (v ph)—to stop and think about things

Digest (v)—to try and understand something

Slang (n)—words that are not officially recognized but are used in conversation

Complex (adj)—very complicated, involving much detail

Reflection (n)—thoughts or memories

Formulate (v)—to organize a plan of action

Appropriate (adj)—the right thing to do

Automatically (adj)—doing something without thinking or deciding

Armed with (idiom)—having a tool, weapon or information to use as needed

Deprive (v)—to keep something from somebody, to not allow

GMAT (General Management Admissions Test) (n)—a test students must take to apply to American universities when pursuing graduate business degrees

Interview (v)—to ask questions, listen for answers, and learn about a person

Feedback (n)—helpful information that is given to help someone improve

Game plan (n)—a plan for the present and future

Juncture (n)—an important point when decisions must be made

Purposely (adv)—to do so by choice or design

Naked (adj)—(not having any clothes on), feeling like something important is missing, feeling vulnerable

Absorb (v)—to take in information, to understand

Ratchet up (idiom)—to increase

Emancipator (n)—something or someone that frees us from slavery

Commute (n)—the journey between home and work

Conference call (n)—a phone or video call involving people at different locations

Retreat (v)—to move away from a situation

Notorious (adj)—known for things that are not positive

Turnover (n)—people leaving a job

Departure (n)—the act of leaving a place or situation

Morale (n)—the attitudes and emotional state of people

Invade (v)—to enter into an enemy's land or space

Rationalize (v)—to give so-so reasons for doing something, sometimes excuses for behavior

Attendee (n)—a person that attends an event or seminar

Lifeline (n)—something that saves a person's life

Migrant workers (n ph)—people that have to leave their home to go and work in other places

Brutal (adj)—very difficult, harsh, unfair

Sub-par (adj)—below average, disappointing

Trespass (v)—to go somewhere you aren't allowed to go

Glitch (n)—a problem in how something operates

Darwinian selection (n ph)—the natural process of eliminating certain members of a species

Micro (adj)—very small, individual

Gradually (adj)—done slowly over a period of time

Creep (v)—to move in a direction at a slow pace

Macro (adj)—very large, the whole, the total population

Shrink (v)—to get smaller

Competitive (adj)—able to participate and do well

Channel (v)—to direct our energies or thoughts, focus

14

Out of balance

"We are the most in-debt, obese, addicted and medicated cohort in U.S. history."

Brené Brown

So we legalize marijuana, enabling more people to get high.

And we have more technology than any time in history, yet, we're not happy.

Why not?

Taiwan, like America, has some issues with discontent (and drugs). At a seminar I was co-leading I spoke with an agent with the Investigative Bureau of the Ministry of Justice. He shared with me that the increase in Taiwan's drug use comes from more young people experimenting with drugs.

So, what's going on? We have prosperity, everything works pretty well, we live long lives, and by economic standards we're wealthier than 95% of the people on Earth.

Psychologist Barry Schwartz gave a TED Talk entitled "The Paradox of Choice", and in it he states;

"There's no question that some choice is better than none, but it doesn't follow from that that more choice is better than some choice. There's some magical amount. I don't know what it is. I'm pretty confident that we have long since passed the point where (more) option(s) improve our welfare."

Here's a link to Barry Schwartz' talk—it's thought-provoking;

Today we have more choices than any society in history ever experienced, with many of those choices right in our hands, yet many of us are confused and out of balance.

The table

A few years ago, during a difficult time in my life, my friend and mentor Bruce Bolen shared with me that healthy people and healthy relationships are like a table with four legs. The four legs are Emotional, Intellectual, Physical and Spiritual, and all four legs need attention for the table to balance. My life was out of balance, and it was taking a toll on my personal and professional life, so I needed to pause and evaluate the areas that were being neglected.

Do you ever feel like your life is out of balance? Do you address that? Do you take time to examine the areas of your life that need adjustment? Most people just grind through life, enduring things—jobs that are dissatisfying, relationships that are incomplete, dreams that remain unfulfilled. We're busy expanding our network of people and processing more information, but while our networks are broad, there's not much depth to them, as in deep relationships.

Do you have a mentor? It's important that we have mentors in our lives, for our careers and for our personal lives. And you need to be a mentor for other people also. By being a mentor for another person, you can "get out of your head", i.e. forget about your issues for a while, and help someone else, which will lift your spirits and theirs.

Mentors are people that guide us and can be sounding boards for what is going on in our life. I actually have four mentors—all of them are older than me, have more life experience, and best of all they have the patience to listen to me and give quality feedback and advice. We all need "sounding boards"—people that help us see things more objectively, since they aren't emotionally involved in our issues. For me, Bruce is one of them, and he led me to examine the table of my life and restore balance. So, I've applied this table metaphor to our digital behavior.

Emotional

One of the more curious aspects of having computers in our hands at all times has been the shift toward isolation and thinking that "**I don't need anybody**". With so much information instantly available we interact less, seldom ask people for help, or seek opportunities to help others—we have everything we need in the palms of our hands—which tends to make us "Lone Wolves".

Not only are we isolating and becoming emotionally disconnected from others, but we're becoming emotionally disconnected from ourselves, not taking time to fully examine "Why do I feel this way?" When we're sad, lonely, angry, depressed or confused our narcotic has become the device, which temporarily distracts us from our emotions, but never really gets to the root causes. We have a thousand Facebook friends, but few who know us deeply, so the emotional leg of our table is short.

Regarding others, we've gone from interdependence to independence, fraying the interpersonal fabric that holds us together as a community. Many times, right in my neighborhood, I've watched people wander in circles, phone in hand, looking at a screen with the address of the Sunny Hills pineapple cake store. The online information is misleading because while the address says Minsheng Road, the store is actually one street behind Minsheng. It's confusing—the address says one thing, but reality says another—and yet, the wanderers circle about, looking at the screen, and refusing to ask for directions ("I don't need anybody"). Often, I'm standing right there, and I know where it is. Sometimes I've asked people if they're looking for Sunny Hills, and yes, they are. So, I tell them where it is—and in all cases it's a pleasant exchange, sometimes leading to a conversation. (Note: men are notorious for not asking for directions—as if it were a sign of weakness.)

These encounters are the tiny threads of emotional connection that we're slowly eradicating with our "I don't need anybody" phone reliance. Our phones reinforce our fear of speaking to others—conversing is a skill we are losing—so we avoid talking and avoid people, especially strangers.

We would do well to remember Jesus' parable of the Good Samaritan (Luke 10:30-37). In this short story, a man needs help, two people think they are too busy to help him, and so they avoid him. A third man comes along, sees the problem, and helps the man.

This is the example we should live by—seeking to help, rather than seeking to avoid. This is how we connect with others, and strengthen our emotional leg.

Today, we're busying ourselves with minutia and meaningless motion, reaching over-capacity with digital stimulation and information, rather than spending precious time to connect with others or our inner-selves and examining our emotional health. Ask any therapist and they will tell you that anxiety and depression are at all-time highs—but we've ignored the emotional toll "always on/always on us" has taken.

Is there anybody close enough that you can share your emotional concerns with, and know that they really care? Are they capable of providing safe and quality emotional support? Because we need it more often than we care to admit. And this is not just a one-way street of "I need help"—just as important is that you help others emotionally.

I rarely hear or read in the media about how our digital behavior impacts our emotional well-being. In the past ten years, I don't see that societal emotional health has improved—rates of depression, suicide and a host of other emotional factors have not gotten better. The devices, the Internet, games and social media have not been an emotional health panacea; it's possible that they have increased the severity of our emotional health issues.

A contemporary philosopher that I've tuned into is Alain de Botton. One topic that he has focused on is "Status Anxiety"—the stress we feel when we compare ourselves to our peers. Interestingly, we don't feel much status anxiety toward rich and famous celebrities or athletes. Most of our anxiety (and feelings of inadequacy) originate from envy of people around us, people we consider our equals. Facebook brings this to the forefront, as we are bombarded with photos and posts of what appear to be the great lives our peers are leading. Sometimes we get jealous, sometimes depressed. Here's a link to one of de Botton's videos on this subject;

The good news is you can change this—you're not a victim—you have choices. The first step is to evaluate your emotional well-being, and think critically about the factors that affect it.

Intellectual

Intellectually we have all the information in the world at our fingertips, but are we getting smarter or just processing information, most of which is forgotten within a couple of days? Accumulating information is necessary at times (often with work), but the real exercise of our mind comes when we contemplate ideas then create solutions and futures for ourselves and others. All the information in the world is useless unless it is combined with contemplation and ideas, and then acting on those ideas.

One aspect of Facebook that I've noticed is that most users just want to look at pictures or short comments. That's why a silly selfie will get 200 likes, but an in-depth article on geopolitics will get few readers: we'd rather skim the cream than dive into the deep waters of critical analysis and thinking. And that's sad, because Facebook could be an awesome platform for contemplation and discourse, but it seldom happens. Instead, it's mostly a temporary distraction which morphs into a perpetual distraction with diminishing returns.

Today, I was wondering "Are we more intelligent now, with our phones and tablets?" Studies have shown that within three days you will forget 90% of what you read or hear—unless you write it down and review it. (Other studies have shown greater retention if reading is done with paper books vs. electronic media.) Most of the digital information we're processing is like eating popcorn and cotton candy, not nutritious "intellectual protein and vegetables" that strengthen our reasoning and analytical muscles that lead to healthy debate and better decisions.

Recently I saw a video titled "Here's the one affordable habit ultra-successful people share" that highlighted one habit Mark Zuckerberg, Bill Gates, Warren Buffet, Mark Cuban, Elon Musk and others like them practice: they read a lot of books, books by other successful people, self-improvement and educational subjects. They seek knowledge. How many books (on your own, not required for school) have you read in the last year? Here's the video;

Seek knowledge; it will help you achieve your goals and purpose in life.

In the next chapter we'll examine our physical and spiritual legs.

The Brené Brown quote at the beginning of this chapter comes from this video (link below). It's good. I suggest that you watch it—especially men. (Chinese subtitles available);

Key Words

Legalize (v)—to make something legal, to allow it

Marijuana (n)—a drug that is smoked

High (adj)—feeling happy due to drugs, an altered state

Out of balance (figure of speech)—things are not normal, not at peace, not content, rushed or stressed

Mentor (n)—a person that guides you on life or work issues

Toll (n)—the price we pay

Neglected (adj)—not given enough attention

Endure (v)—to go through or experience something that is not enjoyable, sometimes painful

Dissatisfying (adj)—not pleasing, disappointing

Unfulfilled (adj)—incomplete, not finished

Broad (adj)—wide

Sounding board (n)—somebody that will listen to you with care

Objectively (adv)—to think clearly, logically, unemotionally

Restore (v)—to return to a previous condition or state

Curious (adj)—wanting to know about things

Lone Wolf (n)—a person who does almost everything alone

Narcotic (n)—a drug or substance that alters our state, numbs our senses

Root cause (n)—the main reason something happens, the main cause

Interdependence (n)—two or more people relying on each other over a period of time

Fray (v)—to make loose, to cause disorder

Fabric (n)—the material that is used to make clothes, curtains, tablecloths

Thread (n)—cotton or fiber in a thin string that is used to make fabric

Eradicate (v)—to eliminate, get rid of something

Parable (n)—a short story told to teach a truth or lesson

Over-capacity (adj)—to many/much, more people or things than can fit

Stimulation (n)—something that causes interest or reaction

Precious (adj)—valuable, worth caring for

Therapist (n)—a mental health professional that provides counseling

Anxiety (n)—stress, nervousness, worry

Well-being (n)—the state of our mental and physical health

A host (n)—a lot, many

Panacea (n)—the cure for everything

Severity (n)—how strong something is

Status (n)—feelings about the self that are based upon money, power, position, education

Inadequacy (n)—the state of not enough, too little

Forefront (n)—in an important position, one of the first things to consider

Peer (n)—the people around us with similar jobs, income, education

Jealous (adj)—wishing that you had what someone else had, not happy with another's success

At our fingertips (figure of speech)—able to do very quickly, easily accessible

Geopolitics (n)—current events and international news about countries and governments

Skim the cream (figure of speech)—only look at what's on top, only the quick and easy things

Dive into the deep waters (figure of speech)—to investigate things more, to do research

Discourse (n)—discussion between two or more people, debate, conversation

Perpetual (adj)—keeps happening, forever repeating

Retention (n)—to remember, retain, save

Cotton candy (n)—a sweet treat made of heated sugar

Nutritious (adj)—something (food) that is good for us, healthy

Protein (n)—a food substance that helps to build muscles and strengthen our body

Reasoning (n)—thinking ability, logic

15

Out of balance, Part 2

"By three methods we may learn wisdom: First, by reflection, which is noblest; second, by imitation, which is easiest; and third by experience, which is the bitterest."

Confucius

Physical

Ergonomic studies have shown the detrimental effects of computers—what too much time sitting at a computer does to our bodies, affecting our backs, necks, eyes, hands, wrists and even our cardiovascular health. Only time will tell what the impact is of holding screens close to our eyes, or what having earphones in at all times does to our ears. Here's an article about the problems with children's eyes in Taiwan—**I'm sure that looking at devices a lot doesn't help**;

Our children spend an inordinate amount of time studying, which strains their eyes, then during non-study time they're staring at small screens, often holding them very close to their eyes. Just as bad are adults—I'm stunned how closely people hold phones to their eyes.

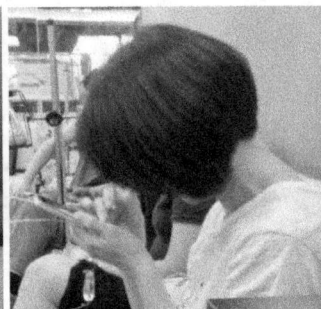

Other studies have shown that muscle development can be delayed with excessive gadget use. This study (link below) examined the impact tablets had on small children, their dexterity and motor skills;

A friend of mine recently noticed that his young daughter was slouching her shoulders and hunching her back, due to excessive tablet viewing. And this same friend had to see a chiropractor due to his own neck pain from too much device time—almost his entire day is spent looking at screens. Without realizing it, our digital addictions are altering our posture.

Speaking of children, we should also be concerned about the content they are exposed to via devices, the Internet and Social media. Cyberspace has become an "anything goes" world, with easy access to disturbing content for children.

Whether children, teens or adults, we don't get enough physical activity when we spend so much time with our devices, surfing the Internet, scrolling social media, playing games or watching videos. We're too sedentary, and this has long-term consequences for our physical well-being. **And we're teaching kids the wrong lessons also, letting them spend hours with screens instead of developing good exercise habits.** What foundation are you laying now for your or your children's long-term physical health?

There's an interesting connection between physical health and emotional well-being: physical activity improves our moods. But as you have probably observed, being engaged with our devices is usually a sedentary activity. We're getting less physical activity with the advent of smartphones and tablets. This is particularly profound with children and teens here in Taiwan. We already curb their physical activity by having them sit in schools all day and cram schools at night and on weekends. Then their lack of physical activity is compounded by so much free time spent on devices.

In America kids also get less physical activity now and spend less time outside playing. When I go home to visit my parents, I go for walks in the neighborhood after dinner, usually 7 pm or so, for an hour or two. In the summer, the sunshine lasts until 9 pm, so most evenings are very nice. My parents live in a typical suburb with plenty of houses, but during my walks, I rarely see any children. No kids riding bikes, none playing basketball in the driveways, none throwing and catching baseballs—no kids outside. Few parents, either. On many walks I don't see anyone! Everybody's inside, looking at screens or playing video games.

Most of the activities that children in America (and to a similar degree in Taiwan) participate in are organized, scheduled and officiated by adults. In the past, kids used to participate in more "unorganized" activities, such as games in the neighborhood, which they learned to organize on their own. That happens less frequently now, as kids bounce between adult-organized activities and screen time, which promotes a highly individualized, self-centered orientation.

What the kids are not learning are character-building organizational skills, fairness in choosing teams and making rules, teamwork, improvisation with less-than-perfect circumstances, the ability to fairly self-officiate games and activities at the street level, basic conflict resolution skills, and how to win and lose gracefully.

My former co-worker at ORTV, Josh Mooney applied a time limit on device usage for his two sons, who were six and eight years-old when they lived in Taiwan. The boys had a 30-minute-a-day limit on their phone and tablet usage—only on Saturday and Sunday (no device time during the school week). The best part about this is that Josh assigned them the responsibility of self-monitoring the amount of time they spent on their devices; they had to keep track of their digital activity. This taught the boys two things: discipline in device usage, and accountability for their time. It's a parenting technique that many adults should try.

For adults here in Taiwan, the physical activity landscape isn't much better, since most adults sit in offices all day, which induces physical and mental lethargy. By the end of the work day, it's easier to spend time on our devices than go and exercise.

It's a good thing we have national health insurance.

So, how is your physical leg of the Life Balance Table looking? Does your digital behavior (and your children's) encourage more or less physical activity?

I go to a Chinese medical clinic near my apartment to get acupuncture and a massage for my shoulder, elbow and finger (too much computer time at work!) One night I said to my doctor, Henry, "Every time I come here this place is so crowded, and it seems to be many of the same people—why?" "They're depressed", he replied. "They come here, get some attention, acupuncture, a massage, and come back tomorrow."

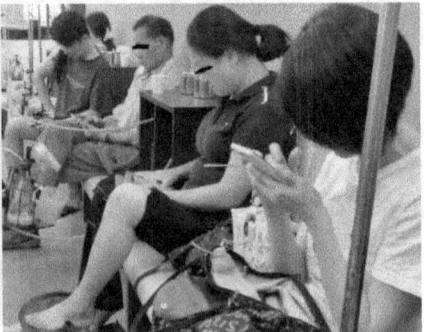

Spiritual

For thousands of years people have prayed, meditated and worshipped individually or in groups. They've studied ancient scriptures, practiced rituals and learned from teachers and elders. Such practices can bring about peace and understanding during life's difficult times, and provide a daily guide for dealing with the challenges that come our way. Priests, ministers, elders and counselors within religious organizations can also provide wisdom and guidance.

Today, our "busyness" leaves little time for honoring and nurturing our spiritual nature; little time for contemplating the meaning of life or our purpose for being here. Instead of using free moments to pray, meditate or study spiritual teachings, we opt for digital stimulation, not spiritual contemplation. If you look around, some of the calmest people you encounter are deeply spiritual. They've learned not to be rattled by the daily ups and downs of life. This runs counter to the digital pop culture that bombards our senses non-stop, with its provocative stimuli aimed at getting a reaction from us.

If you take time to cultivate your spiritual leg, it will help you to define your purpose in life—i.e. answer the questions "Why am I here?" and "What should I to do with this gift of life?" Surely we're not here just to make money, buy things, pay bills and have fun.

In Taiwan many people are moving away from their Buddhist or Taoist traditions, while in America many people drift away from Christianity. Whether we're allied with Buddhist, Taoist, Christian, Muslim, Hindu or any other religious tradition, we need to take time to address how our spiritual lives can benefit from more time and attention. (If you're an atheist or agnostic, then this leg of your Life Balance Table might be called the Wisdom leg.) We all need some wisdom, usually from elders or knowledgeable people, because none of us has all the answers. Elders offer wisdom plus calmness in times of trouble, so we can't just rely on our own knowledge—it's limited.

In some ways, our phone has become our church or temple, and the content from our devices has become the holy verses and scriptures. If you are religious or spiritual, is your device replacing God in your life? But digital worship is an empty religion, since it is always changing, with little or no moral authority in our life. As a result, we discount the spiritual leg of our Life Balance Table. We may try to replace it with online advice like "Ten Ways to be Motivated", "8 Tips for Finding Happiness" or "Five Things to Eat Today". The Internet supplies these guides daily, then we forget most of them in a week.

Spirituality is a daily practice—it requires a consistent effort. I pray every day, several times a day. Three or four times a week I stop by a nearby church, go in and sit down for 15 or 20 minutes, be quiet and pray. We need stillness—a time of peace and quiet to reflect, a time of no distraction to meditate. I'm far from a perfect Christian—I'm incredibly flawed—which is the reason I need this time. It calms me, it helps me to sort out things in my life, and I try to listen for what God is telling me.

I meet many students, teachers and business people in Taiwan. During my conversations with them one of the questions I ask is "Do you go to a church, or a temple, or some religious organization?" It's surprising how few do, particularly the under-40 crowd. And yet, many of them are not happy. I try to encourage them to pursue some religious practice or spiritual exploration. They don't have the answers for their lives—and I don't have all the answers for their lives, either. But I know there is great wisdom that they are missing by not addressing the spiritual leg of their Life Balance Table.

The wisdom of the phone

184

Sir Ken Robinson talked about Carl Jung's observations on the importance of religion ("spirituality" according to Robinson) in a talk delivered at the Dalai Lama Center for Peace and Education a few years ago:

"And I think the reason so many people get depressed and lost is that they have lost the connection with themselves. They have no sense of purpose.

Carl Jung said this; he said that in his thirty years of professional practice, he said there wasn't a single person who came to see him whose malaise, he said, couldn't in the end, be attributed to a loss of faith in religion. Now, I don't think he meant, and I certainly don't mean in quoting him, organized religion. I think the word I would use, and perhaps he would've accepted, would be spirituality, a sense of your spirit. But he said, in the end, nobody either got well without regaining a sense of spiritual connection."

Here's the link to the video (this quote is at 41:20 to 41:52);

Note: Carl Jung is one of the giants in the field of psychology. Here is his Wikipedia page:

Another benefit of addressing our spiritual leg is that it provides us with community, in the form of small groups of people that share the same beliefs, and also provide support and advice during difficult times. It's been said that we are like the five people closest to us—we become like them. So, which five people are closest to you? Do they make you better, or keep you in the same life pattern? What are their practices, and do you learn valuable lessons from them? Do you help them to improve?

I have "spiritual brothers and sisters" that I share faith with, and we also share our problems (and possible solutions). We worship together, pray together, and we each have permission to offer "tough love" to each other—we allow correction from the others, because they often see things more clearly than I do. Do you have spiritual brothers or sisters that have permission to give you needed, sometimes difficult, feedback? You need this—you need people that have permission to hold you accountable for your actions and decisions.

If your digital behavior prevents you from having five people close to you, are your device and social media practices filling this void and making you better?

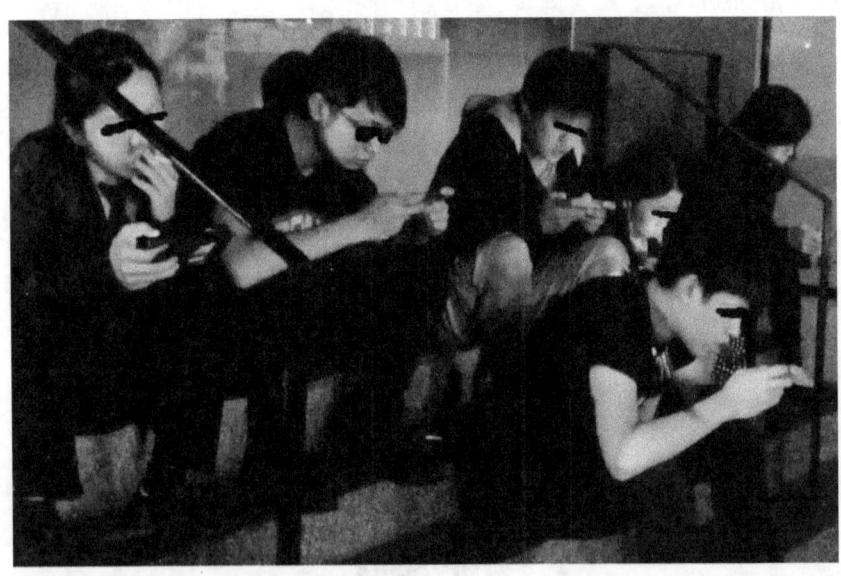

Who are your five closest friends, and how do they influence you?

Shifting the paradigm, balancing our table

If it sounds like I'm a resistor to technology, I'm not; I had an iPhone 3GS given to me eight years ago, when only 10% of the people in Taipei had smartphones. I'd be on the MRT with my iPhone, and people looked on with curiosity, wondering about it. And then devices, the Internet, social media, videos and games swept over us like a tsunami in a blink of an eye. Most of us aren't good at managing all of this, causing the tables of our lives to get out of balance. The technology isn't going away—it's only going to increase—so we need to pause, step back, and look at the legs of our Life Balance Table to see what needs attention.

How do we do that? Try these;

- Get a mentor. You need one, for your life, for your career (And you be a mentor to another person)
- Identify one person that you can connect with on a deep, emotional level
- Switch from endless scrolling of fluff items to in-depth reading of knowledge material
- Turn off the phone or tablet and go exercise
- Join a church, temple, or some religious or spiritual group
- Take time each day to pray or meditate

Combine these steps with setting goals and defining your purpose in life. I guarantee you that your life will improve.

Now, here are two extreme steps for changing your daily digital behavior;

1. Take a 30-day social media diet. Deactivate your Facebook account, turn off the LINE groups. The first couple days will feel strange, but you'll survive, and it gets easier. You'll find that you have more free time, less anxiety and you'll get more sleep. You don't have to quit forever, just 30 days. You can do anything for 30 days, so I know you can do this.

2. Take a 30-day diet from your smartphone (and tablet). Remove your SIM card from your smartphone and put it into a basic cellphone. You can still communicate via phone calls and text messages. You'll have more free time, less anxiety and <u>you'll get more sleep</u>.

Impossible?

No, these digital diets are not impossible. I've done both, a couple of times, and it shifted my paradigm of device and social media interaction. The long-term impact has been a sensible readjustment of how I use digital media as a valuable, managed tool that enhances my life, not a crutch that dominates my existence.

In the Sir Ken Robinson talk that I referenced earlier, he shared this quote by the Dalai Lama;

"To be born at all is a miracle; now, what will you do with it?"

Key Words

Ergonomic (adj)—studying how work affects the human body

Detrimental (adj)—a bad influence, a negative impact

Cardiovascular (adj)—dealing with the condition of the heart

Only time will tell (figure of speech)—we will find out later

Inordinate (adj)—to many of something, more than the normal situation requires

Dexterity (n)—the ability to move our body, especially our hands a free and helpful way

Slouch (v)—leaning the head and neck forward

Hunch (v)—leaning the shoulders forward

Chiropractor (n)—a medical professional that makes adjustments to the skeletal system

Posture (n)—how we stand or sit, the position of our body

Anything goes (figure of speech)—no rules

Sedentary (adj)—too much sitting around, not moving, lazy

Foundation (n)—the base of something such as a house or building

Lay (v)—to put down something, to put it flat on the ground

Curb (v)—to limit or shorten something

Suburb (n)—the residential area outside of the city

Driveway (n)—a place where cars are parked (usually next to a house)

Officiate (v)—to enforce the rules during a game, to decide on plays

Individualized (adj)—made for the individual, limited to one person

Self-centered (adj)—focusing only on the self, caring only about "me"

Orientation (n)—the situation or how things are organized

Improvisation (n)—the ability to think quickly, to work well without perfect factors

At the street level (figure of speech)—not fancy or luxurious, simple, common

Gracefully (adj)—acting with style, class, honor

Apply (v)—to put something into practice, to use something

Assign (v)—to give work to, to tell someone to do something

Keep track (idiom)—to count how many or how much of something

Landscape (n)—the situation, the environment

Induce (v)—to cause something to happen, to get start something

Lethargy (n)—the feeling of laziness, no energy

Acupuncture (n)—Chinese medicine practice of using needles to ease pain

Meditate (v)—to be quiet, sit still, to relax in thought

Scripture (n)—writings that religions are based upon

Ritual (n)—something that is done as a way to remember or signify something

Nurture (v)—to care for, to help grow

Opt for (idiom)—to choose

Rattled by (idiom)—something causes upset, worry or stress

Runs counter (idiom)—is the opposite of something

Stimuli (n)—small things that get our attention

Cultivate (v)—to help grow, to develop

Move away from (something) (figure of speech)—not be involved with, not do anymore

Allied with (idiom)—belong to, connected with

Atheist (n)—a person that believes there is no God, does not believe religions

Agnostic (n)—a person that doesn't know if there is a God

Moral (adj)—the right things to do, the right decision-making beliefs

Discount (v)—to give less value to something, to think it's not important

Stillness (n)—being quiet, sitting still, not thinking about things

Flawed (adj)—not perfect, having weaknesses or defects

Permission (n)—the right to do or say something

Tough love (n ph)—being honest with people in order to help them

Tsunami (n)—a giant wave of water

Shift the paradigm—to change the way of thinking and operating, to change our understanding

Fluff (n)—silly, unimportant things

In-depth (adj)—many details, much research

Guarantee (v)—to promise something, a sure thing

Deactivate (v)—to halt the operation of something, to halt participation

16

The Fifth Leg

"We all have finite time and energy"

Randy Pausch, from "The Last Lecture"

In the last chapter I discussed the Life Balance Table, and how our digital behavior can cause it to be unbalanced. There's another leg I need to address.

Energy

I've taken my mentor Bruce Bolen's four-legged table and added a fifth leg—Energy--right in the middle of the table that makes it stronger. Energy affects the other four legs, so it's important to manage our energy properly, or else our batteries will get drained.

We have Emotional Energy, which is spent during periods of stress, frustration, excitement and elation. Intellectual Energy is spent processing and responding to information. With a constant stream of stimuli and information coming our way from our devices and social media, we don't fully realize the extra emotional and intellectual energy drain we're experiencing. The reason we are often emotionally and intellectually fatigued is because we're digitally overwhelmed, every day, leading to a loss of patience and kindness.

Spiritual energy is either being drained or not replenished when we don't address our spiritual needs due to constant distraction, causing loss of hope. But the most insidious drain devices and social media have on us is our physical energy. Human beings by nature take the path of least resistance. Our phones and tablets provide the easiest route to distraction from our current state, leading to passivity and ambivalence. Playing with our devices requires minimal physical effort—basically just sitting and staring—which degrades our physical well-being.

It's amazing how many people I see, young and old, sitting for hours, staring at screens instead of being actively engaged in physical activity that would increase their energy levels. In some ways, our internal battery mirrors the battery icon on our devices, as it slowly decreases with more usage. And we get less sleep due to our digital behavior, which drains our energy.

Staying up late at night, using our devices, certainly cuts into our sleep time—and the late night screen time prevents us from falling asleep by activating our eyes and brain. But, something few of us realize is that our digital activity throughout the day gobbles up productive time, pushing back our bed time. We often have to stay up late to get things done because of the time we spent during the day bouncing in and out of box 3 (those "urgent", but not important digital activities). Remember—the more time you spend in box 3 during the day, the less sleep you will get. Then we go to work the next day in a zombie-like trance—which lowers our productivity, which prevents goal achievement. And we keep doing this, every day.

Have your energy levels—Emotional, Intellectual, Spiritual and Physical—increased or decreased with the rise in your digital activity?

Are we more enthusiastic about life? Look around at people using their phone and right after they finish using their phone; do they look energetic? No, they don't—they look tired. And after a minute or two, they check the phone again. It all drains our internal batteries—and we don't realize how this keeps us stuck in life.

Feel the energy!

For Taiwan, there is a danger in this energy drain creating ambivalence and passivity—a sense of disempowerment and detachment. The next few years will be challenging for Taiwan, and we need all the human capital available—creating, collaborating and cooperating—to sustain the great society that we enjoy. We don't have the luxury of sitting back, killing time, thinking prosperity will simply last forever. We need to work together, and we need to work with the rest of the world—that's not going to happen if a significant percentage of the population is hanging out in box 3 (Urgent, Not Important) and box 4 (Not Urgent, Not Important).

Combined, Singapore and Hong Kong have about 13,000,000 people. The combined area of both is 1,800 square kilometers. Taiwan has a population of 23,500,000, and 36,200 square kilometers. So, Taiwan has nearly double the population of these two, and 20 times the area, plus more natural resources, an educated population and financial resources. There's no reason Taiwan can't compete if our energy is channeled in the right direction.

Special note: here is a link to *The Last Lecture* by Randy Pausch (with Chinese subtitles):

Key Words

Elation (n)—extreme happiness and joy

Overwhelmed (adj)—having too much of something, more than we can handle

Insidious (adj)—having a negative effect without being noticed

The path of least resistance (figure of speech)—the easiest thing to do

Internal (adj)—inside

Mirror (v)—to be the same, look or do the same

Activate (v)—to cause activity or action, to start something

Zombie-like (adj)—having little energy, little emotion

Energetic (adj)—having energy, excitement

Disempowerment (n)—a feeling of powerlessness, hopelessness

Human capital (n ph)—the talents and skill of individuals or a group of people

Sustain (v)—to keep something going

The real cost of things

Most of us don't fully understand energy—how we manage it, how it is drained—because we don't critically think about energy allocation. Here's an example: car ownership, which is a far bigger energy drain than most people realize.

Intellectual energy; dealing with the legalities, insurance and other regulations required. Emotional energy; dealing with anger that occurs during driving, frustration when repairs are needed, stress in unexpected costs. Physical energy; the number of hours that you need to work to pay the car payment, insurance, gasoline, repairs and parking.

For instance, in America, when you add in all the costs of car ownership, it's about $1,000 a month. That's a lot of energy for most employees to devote to transportation. They're literally working half the month so they can drive to work.

That's just one item in the mix of life. Now, apply that sort of critical thinking to the optional areas of life that you participate in. In chapter 12 I mentioned all my online accounts—dealing with those takes energy. For instance, I've spent 8 years and thousands of hours on Facebook, and I'm not sure what return I've gotten from that energy expense. So, be wise with your energy allocation.

17

Underlying Causes

"The good is the enemy of the best."

Dr. Henry Cloud, *Integrity*

To understand our choices and actions, it's important to look at how our character and personalities are shaped. What may be some of the root causes of our digital behavior?

Shyness

The price of "I'm shy" is missed opportunity.

"I'm shy" is something that I often hear from people. But shyness is not a genetic trait; it is a learned behavior that we can unlearn. During my first two years in Taiwan, I taught many young children at several kindergartens, and I can tell you that 4 and 5-year-olds are not shy. They are full of energy, imagination and loud voices.

That was you, many years ago.

But the education system and society takes this energy and imagination and puts a lid on it, conforming our personalities until we all fall in line. We are literally socialized to be shy. Our systems don't teach kids to engage; we teach them to shy away from taking chances. Inherent in this training is fear of the risk of failure, and we learn early that there are big penalties for failure. So, we go into our shyness shells.

In Taiwan, English is taught strictly as a writing and reading discipline, primarily for testing purposes, with little to no emphasis on speaking the language. The emphasis on testing actually discourages teachers from promoting spoken communication, since speaking is not quantified—thus, removing spoken communications as a goal. For ten years they study English, but few students feel comfortable speaking the language. (English is just part of the education system, but I think it's indicative of the emphasis on testing and conformity. This tends to discourage creativity, risk taking and communications—and encourages shyness.)

So, then we have pervasive shyness that is now facilitated by our phones and tablets. Staring at our devices is a socially acceptable way of maintaining shyness; a convenient way of not talking or even looking at anybody. Ask yourself, "Am I using my phone to maintain my shyness?"

The good news is that shyness is not in our DNA—it's a learned behavior that can be changed. I've worked with people who told me "I used to be so shy", but they moved beyond that.

One of those people is a former co-worker at ORTV, Sandy. Sandy spent over ten years working on the Studio Classroom TV show, hosting a popular daily segment. Sandy is a dynamic, energetic and multi-lingual professional who is the epitome of the words "Awesome Teacher". But Sandy told me that when she was a teenager, she was very, very shy, and hardly ever spoke. She worked on that, grew out of her shyness, and has enjoyed a successful career as a presenter and communicator. In addition to working on TV and visiting schools, Sandy traveled to other countries representing ORTV, conducting seminars and workshops.

You can do this, too! The benefit is that your life and career can blossom if you shed this label about yourself. If you hold onto shyness, then life may become a string of missed opportunities.

Seeing more than words

One soft skill that we diminish if we rely on texting and messaging, rather than speaking and engaging, is the ability to "**read**" **people**. So much of communications is in facial expressions, **body language**, tone and speed, even pauses. Successful people are good at "reading" people—i.e. **interpreting** the messages the person is sending, beyond the words.

I don't need anybody

In Chapter 14 regarding the emotional leg of our "Life Balance Table", I mentioned "I don't need anybody", so I want to examine this deeper here.

As I wrote this book I considered that maybe people just don't like people. We may like the people closest to us, but beyond our close circle, maybe deep down we just don't want to deal with people. Which then led to "maybe we're just tired of people"—that can happen in a crowded city. One convenient way to avoid people is to focus on our devices—we can appear to be busy that way, with our body language sending out the message "Don't bother me".

I call this "people fatigue". Then we may isolate in our devices, which leads some of us to the attitude of "I don't need anybody"—I have everything I need in my hand.

I get it on the people possibly not liking people thing. People can be **ma fan** 麻煩. I can be ma fan.

"Ah, but my phone is never ma fan, my tablet never gives me a headache, my device is my **trouble-free** friend."

If you wish to achieve your goals in life, you need to deal with people—strangers, people that you don't like, people who have very different ideas than you. Successful people learn how to communicate with all types and do it gracefully. Yes, they use their devices for some of this, but they also use their eyes, mouths and ears—especially their ears, to listen and engage. If we just focus on our phones and tablets, we block out many of the challenges and learning opportunities that come our way each day.

What's overlooked in "I don't need anybody" is that others may need you. We don't think about this often—how we may be of service to others. Our **device-centric** lives pretty much revolve around "What's in it for me?" or "What do I get out of it?"

What we miss by focusing on our devices and on ourselves, is that giving and helping others is much more **rewarding** in the long-run, leading to deeper more meaningful relationships. By helping others we evolve into greater beings who experience much more contentment and joy.

For many of us, Shyness and "I don't need anybody" define our comfort zone. Comfort zones are nice, cozy places for us to relax. But to truly grow, we need to step out of our comfort zone.

John Hambrick is an author who wrote a book titled *Move Toward the Mess*, which encourages us to move outside of our comfort zones. Why would we want to do that? I recently watched an interview he gave, and he neatly summarizes it in this quote:

*"We love our comfort zones. There's nothing wrong with comfort zones—they're a great place to recuperate, but they're not a great place to live, because nothing much happens in your comfort zone. And if you spend too much time there, it starts to get boring. **We will never meet the best version of ourselves inside our comfort zone.**"*

Here's the interview, with this quote at 19:00—30;

We're bored

Never before have we had such complete entertainment systems available to us in the palms of our hands. To alleviate our boredom we've become addicted to being entertained.

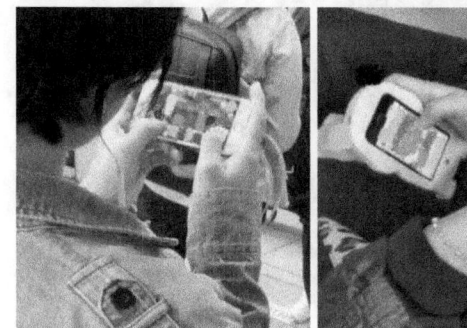

So now we carry our entertainment with us. I continue with John Hambrick, whom I quoted in the previous section. He mentioned comfort zones, and how they get boring if we just stay in them. How do we usually deal with boredom? He says in that interview;

"A lot of people think the opposite of boredom is entertainment. But, I don't think that's true, not in any sort of meaningful way. Entertainment, of course, is fun—but it doesn't last for very long. I think the real solution to boredom is being engaged." (quote at 25:50—26:07 of the interview)

Entertainment is fine, in moderation. But it's temporary. This addiction to entertainment is not restricted to Taiwan: in America, I see masses of people addicted to sports, wasting their lives watching sports, every day—hours and hours. It's how Americans entertain themselves today.

Ask yourself, "Am I relying too much on my device, the Internet or social media to entertain me?" Then evaluate if this is a satisfactory, long-term solution to chronic boredom. If boredom is chronic, change your life strategy, and find alternatives to the need for constant entertainment.

It's a networking world

With Facebook, LinkedIn, LINE, Twitter and others, social networking has become an obsession for many of us. It's all about accumulating as many names as possible, believing quantity is better than quality. Our networks are broad, but not deep. We "know" lots of people, but know few of them very well. This seems like a contradiction of "I don't need anybody", as it reveals that we do need others. But it's needing others *and* keeping them at a safe distance.

Many professional advice articles advise people to "network" in order to facilitate their career, which drives much of this behavior. In his book, *Integrity*, Dr. Henry Cloud differentiates between networking and alliance building;

"Alliance building is key to success and leadership. It is more than 'networking', which is often just a synonym of leeching. Alliances are about creating leverage to take what you do to a multiple."

What Dr. Cloud was talking about in his quote is that in most cases we don't bring value to the networking relationship—we just seek to take advantage of the other person's success. A true networking relationship is reciprocal—we don't just take, but we also provide some value to others. That is alliance building, which is creating long-term relationships, not just seeking our own temporary gain.

How did we get to this point?

The problem for most people is that nobody showed us how to network properly. Today's "networking" primarily consists of digital efforts, which are relatively passive—and produces so-so results. Most people are too "spread out"—not focused, trying to have as many contacts as possible with minimal effort. This is diffuse, weak, and usually doesn't produce much return. The ideal networking technique is to blend targeted digital networking with interpersonal communications—not so easy, since it requires more effort, but produces greater results.

Instead of trying to gather as many digital contacts as possible, write down a list of ten people that you would like to network with. Then focus on those ten people. Take time to get to know them, provide some service to them (such as helpful information), write constructive letters/emails to them that show thought and effort, talk with them on the phone and meet with them in person. This will set you apart from the dozens or even hundreds of people that digitally cycle through their life and mean nothing to them.

Generational differences

How each generation uses technology is quite different, and how each generation interacts with the world around them is also quite different. Nobody's wrong—just different. Regardless of generation, the basics of human interaction remain: two people looking at, talking and listening to each other.

Nobody cares to talk to grandma

As a foreign English teacher living here in Taiwan for 13 years, the impression I get from the Under-40 crowd is this;

"We don't need you—the computer in my hand is all I need. The phone or tablet allows us to be international. We have Google Translate, we can watch videos from anywhere, see photos of anything in the world in an instant. We can text, message or Skype around the world at any time, and if we want to listen to any language it's all right here in my hand. The world is in my hand. Why are you here?"

Ouch. Have I become obsolete?

(Note: "The world is in my hand" thinking is true not just in Taiwan, but in America and many other places. Unfortunately, it's a mindset that keeps us insular.)

We may be able to access the world, but it doesn't necessarily make us more international. Only by interacting on a personal basis do we really grow beyond the boundaries of our

206

present status. We need **diversity** to expand our interpersonal skills and to deepen our understanding of different cultures. Skimming information from my phone may give me some knowledge, but it's not the same as interacting on a personal level with people from other parts of the world.

Do we engage with and learn from people from different cultures . . .

. . . or do we avoid them?

Here's an analogy: I can read all about golf, and watch lots of tournaments and instructional videos on my tablet or phone. But it's unlikely that I'll get better at golf. The only way I will get better is to go to the practice golf range, hit lots of practice shots, have a golf coach analyze my swing and instruct me, and then play many rounds of golf on a real golf course. Then, I will become a better golfer—by doing, not just watching. I need to engage the game.

Whether in Cambodia or India or even Taiwan, it only takes a moment to connect, just a smile to build a bridge. We need to reach out wherever we are—not run from engagement.

I could have spent the past thirteen years in Pittsburgh, reading all about Taiwan, looking at pictures of Taiwan, watching videos and eating at the many Chinese restaurants owned by Taiwan ex-pats there. But that would not have been anywhere near the learning experience of actually living in Taiwan and engaging the people here.

By engaging the people I learn about the culture, the traditions, the attitudes and the nuances. From this direct interaction I have learned how to communicate, negotiate and compromise on a whole different level—a much more effective level than if I had only read articles or watched videos on my phone.

Model United Nations students (Nini, Yilia, Trevor) at Nanshan HS (top photo), and Civil Service Development Institute leaders (Claire, Evelyn, Janet, Frank). Both groups seek to be bridges and connect with people around the world.

Why does this matter?

At Taiwan's Civil Service and Development Institute (CSDI) 行政院人事行政總處公務人力發展中心 during the past several years, I've trained over 500 Taiwan government mid-and-high-level employees on attending international conferences, giving presentations, participating in **APEC** meetings and advanced-level English. Throughout all of these seminars, the **theme** is interaction and engagement—meeting, greeting and speaking with foreigners on a professional level. I've also trained corporate employees and students in these skills, so they can better represent their companies and schools.

This is how the world sees Taiwan—through the people that engage—whether they are government servants, corporate employees, or students that participate in Model United Nations. Now, more than ever, we need to engage at a personal level. "The world is in my hands" thinking doesn't make us more international or capable communicators—it's just pseudo-internationalism—kind of like Americans getting Chinese symbols tattooed on their bodies; superficial; not the real deal.

Yes, technology has its role in learning things about the world, but the difference-maker is actively speaking, listening and communicating in person at greater levels.

Wage stagnation

For at least 15 years wages have stagnated here in Taiwan. The consequence of that is many young people have become frustrated and ultimately ambivalent about their future prospects. Wage stagnation demotivates, removes a sense of urgency and leads to a state of "existence only". 小確幸 expresses this state of mind perfectly—all I want (or can expect) is a little bit of happiness—so, we settle in our comfort zone. For many young people this existence consists of;

- I have cheap health care
- I have cheap transportation (motorcycles, MRT, buses)
- I live with my parents, so my expenses are low
- I have all the entertainment I need in the palm of my hand

While that may be a recipe for a simple life and seems okay, over time it kills ambition—resulting in the focus on devices, with little planning for the future. I worry that we're becoming lax, "settling" for the status quo, assuming that prosperity will last forever, and thinking "this is good enough".

Dr. Henry Cloud discusses "good" in another section of *Integrity*;

*"To let go of something that isn't working is a sine qua non of healthy people and high performers, as we have seen. But, that is entry level to the field of successful living and achieving. The high performers go a step further. They let go of things that are working, if they are not the best things. What that means is that they are able to let go of things that take up time, energy, and resources that may be good, and even profitable, but are keeping them from the best things. **The good is the enemy of the best**."*

Are you settling for "good"? You have a choice in this. Continue the same behavior, and expect little change over the next several decades. Or, examine the behavior, adjust this behavior for effectiveness, set goals and define a meaningful purpose for your life. We can't assume that somebody else, some government agency, or some magician will make things better. Don't just keep drifting non-stop in cyberspace, even if it seems "good" today, because it ransoms your future.

Consider these three questions:

1. What did you do last week?
2. What did you do this week?
3. What will you do next week?

Most people struggle to remember last week, this week is a busy blur, and next week is "I don't know". This is why we must be vigilant with our time and conscious of our plans if we are to change the course of our life.

The bigger question is "Where will you be in a year?"

For the leaders of Taiwan, it's quite simple: wage stagnation = no hope. With no hope, the young people of Taiwan lose faith in the future, and many of our best and brightest young adults leave or want to leave, taking with them energy and ability. This has created an exodus of top talent to other countries. What future is there in that?

If wage stagnation continues, the younger generations will follow their phones, not their leaders, resigned to "a little bit of happiness", or hopping on planes to greener pastures.

Two other notes for leaders:

1. Wage stagnation also affects the quality of foreigners that Taiwan is able to attract and retain. One of the things that has helped the American economy has been the contribution of immigrants at all levels, including high levels; Jony Ive (Apple), Sergey Brin (Google), Elon Musk and Jerry Yang. And W. Edwards Deming contributed

greatly to Japan's economic miracle. Is there room at Taiwan's table for creative outsiders? If not, the top talent goes elsewhere.

2. The pension system isn't just a math problem—it could become a huge social divide. Many young workers know they will never reach income levels that are handed out in pensions. Plus, billions of NT$ each year simply go into savings, rather than being spent, which doesn't stimulate the economy. Lack of spending contributes to wage stagnation, which demotivates young workers, killing their ambition with low wages and a bleak economic future. Instead of aiming high, life becomes "How cheap can I live?"—not the mindset we need to build our future.

Summary

In this chapter I've identified six root causes of our current digital behavior. I'm sure you can think of others. My goal is to get us thinking and talking about these, along with some of the other issues that I've raised in this book.

Regarding "Shyness", it can be overcome—but only if you want to overcome it. There are costs to maintaining shyness, and there are benefits in overcoming it. It's not easy, but you can do it.

With "I Don't Need Anybody", we have the paradox of distancing ourselves from others, yet inherently needing connection, attention and approval. We want love, but on our terms. Eventually we learn that love and life are messy, and people let us down. Guess what—we let people down, too. The sooner we accept our flaws and the flaws of others, the sooner we grow.

How we handle "We're Bored" is to step out of our comfort zone. Choose to engage people and your boredom will be alleviated. Help others—you won't be bored, and you won't be lonely.

Here's a tip for managing this "Networking World": Each day do one networking task that will help you to reach your goals. Write a meaningful email, make a phone call or visit one of the ten people that you wish to network with. In a year you will have made 365 efforts at connecting on a deeper level with important people. Do this each day and you will reach your goals.

Understand the "Generational Differences" and think outside the phone. We are losing our ability to talk with others. Interacting face-to-face is paramount not only for personal growth, but world peace. Does that sound like an exaggeration? Consider this: Why do countries need ambassadors and diplomats? Digital tools help, but meeting, speaking and listening to diverse groups of people is how we all become bridges between cultures. You be the bridge.

"Wage Stagnation" has been in place here for so long. You can't change it, but you do have the power to change how you deal with it. Evaluate what you need to do to give yourself as many options in life as possible—and then get to work on that.

We choose to be islands or bridges. The consequence of our choice is how others respond to us—with their own choice to be an island or a bridge in return.

Engagement starts with you.

Key Words

Missed opportunity (n ph)—an opportunity that we did nothing with, let it pass

Genetic (adj)—being determined by our genes, our biological makeup

Trait (n)—something that identifies us, part of our being

Learned behavior (n ph)—something that we were taught or conditioned to do

Unlearn (v)—to forget, to stop doing or thinking

Put a lid on it (figure of speech)—to cover, to limit

Conform (v)—to follow the rules, be like everyone else

Fall in line (figure of speech)—to behave the same

Socialized (v)—how our personalities are formed and affected by others

Inherent (adj)—already within us, part of our being

Shell (n)—a safe place, protective cover

Primarily (adv)—the main thing, most important

Emphasis (n)—importance

Quantify (v)—able to be counted or scored

Indicative (adj)—an example of something, to show a pattern

Pervasive (adj)—everywhere, widespread

Facilitate (v)—to help something happen

DNA (n)—contains our genetic material, the makeup of who we are

Multi-lingual (adj)—speaking many different languages

Epitome (n)—the best example

Blossom (v)—to bloom like a flower, to shine

Shed (a) label (figure of speech)—giving up a way that we are, changing things about us

Read people (v ph)—to see and understand beyond the spoken word

Body language (n ph)—the information and messages our physical manner sends

Interpret (v)—to understand different meanings of things

Ma fan (Chinese 麻煩) (adj)—problematic, difficult

Trouble-free (adj)—not having any problems

Device-centric (adj)—focused on devices

Rewarding (adj)—great benefit

Alternative (n)—something different, an option

Differentiate (v)—to show how two or more things are different

Leech (v)—to take or use for one's own interests

Reciprocal (adj)—doing something for somebody who has done something for you

Spread out (adj)—too busy to do a good job on anything

Diffuse (adj)—not strong, energy that is not directed or focused

Blend (v)—to mix together two things, usually to make them better

Set you apart (figure of speech)—make you different from others

Cycle through (idiom)—things that come and go, temporary

Generational (adj)—differences based on age, usually in increments of 15-20 years

Obsolete (adj)—not useful anymore

Insular (adj)—not interested in outside things, narrow-minded, isolated

Diversity (n)—a variety of things, different qualities

Analogy (n)—an example that is similar, to describe something in different terms

Round (n)—18 holes of golf

Nuance (n)—small things that indicate differences

APEC (Asia-Pacific Economic Cooperation) (n)—an group that promotes economic growth for its members

Theme (n)—the style of something, a pattern

Model United Nations (MUN) (n)—a student group that follows United Nations practices

Pseudo (adj)—not real, a fake

Demotivate (v)—to take away energy and motivation, remove hope

Recipe (n)—a formula, a plan of operating

Ambition (n)—the desire to achieve things, to accomplish goals

Sine qua non (Latin) (n)—an essential condition or requirement

Magician (n)—a person that does magic acts, entertains people

Ransom (v)—to pay for something that has been taken away

Blur (n)—something that moves quickly which can't be clearly seen

Exodus (n)—many people leaving a place, usually at the same time

Resigned to (idiom)—having to accept something, no choice

Hop on (idiom)—get on

Greener pastures (n ph)—a place with more opportunity

Overcome (v)—to move past obstacles and problems, move forward

Messy (adj)—disorganized, not tidy, not clean

Let (someone) down (figure of speech)—to disappoint them

Exaggeration (n)—something more than it really is, not being truthful

Ambassador (n)—a person that represents a country overseas

Diplomat (n)—a person that conducts meetings and negotiations for their country

Who's here in Taiwan?

Here are Foreign Resident statistics (as of 5/31/16) from the National Immigration Agency—Total and top ten countries;

Total—653,432

1. Indonesia 223,535
2. Vietnam 169,604
3. Philippines 128,468
4. Thailand 64,076
5. Malaysia 17,758
6. Japan 13,675
7. USA 10,104
8. Korea 3,990
9. Canada 2,158
10. UK 1,858

(Link to NIA statistics)

18

Small changes, big results

"The Internet is not going to save the world"

Bill Gates

I started this book with the question "How can you create a brighter future for yourself, and help make Taiwan better?"

Before reading this book you already had a general idea of <u>what</u> you do on a regular basis with your phone, tablet, social media and the Internet. Hopefully, the issues raised have caused you to take a closer look at your daily digital activity. Knowing what we do is the first step.

Then we need to examine <u>why</u> we do the things we do, and consider the <u>consequences</u> of that behavior. The goal is to get better—it's an ongoing process. The key to getting better is to use critical thinking regarding the digital habits and rituals that we practice every day. Through critical thinking we can determine if they are leading us to fulfill our purpose in life and achieve the goals we have set.

In Chapter 11 I brought up the concept of "connecting the dots". This term first became popular right after 9/11. Investigators realized that certain facts existed prior to the terrorist attacks, and if these facts had been considered together or connected, then the authorities may have been able to prevent the attacks. Instead, they didn't "connect the dots", leading to the events of 9/11.

It's important that we connect the dots in our lives, the bits of information about us that paint a big picture of who we are. I put many links to articles, information and videos in this book is because they are some dots that need to be connected to understand the changes that are happening in society, and what our society is becoming. Individually, different pieces of data don't mean much—but when put together they show a pattern. Connect the dots in your individual life, and then make the choices that you deem necessary to improve things.

As I mentioned in my Introduction, "You're either getting better, staying the same or getting worse." The first and last statuses are obvious, but the cost of staying the same is not understood by most people. If you stay the same, the world will pass you by.

I encourage you to review the boxes in the Urgent/Important Matrix, complete this analysis and be honest with where you spend your time. Then, be sure to complete your goal list. Doing these two exercises will clarify things for you and probably alter your behavior. I don't want you to abandon the technology, but rather sharpen when and how you use it. In most cases it will result in more fulfilling choices, better task execution and higher goal achievement. Small changes often lead to big results.

That's on a personal level. If organizations and companies have employees do these things, they would likely see higher productivity levels, along with having more content workforces with big picture views.

Make sure your Life Balance Table is balanced. By addressing our emotional, intellectual, physical and spiritual aspects we can have a greater sense of peace and contentment in a world that is swirling about us at breathtaking speed. By doing so we can make calmer, wiser choices regarding how we use the finite energy and time we have.

Be present, live in the now, be engaged with others. Look, listen, talk, listen, listen, share. Smile—it's the beginning of interacting, which is the seed of making our future.

Our devices, the Internet, Facebook, LINE and all the other technology we use are fantastic tools that enable us to do many things. But, we need balance, and we need to manage the technology, not let it overtake our lives. When we let that happen, we become separated, isolated.

Our greatest joys come from engaging others—we live, we learn, we cry, we laugh, we grow when we engage others, when we help others. You may not realize this, but people need you. Yes, people need YOU. Taiwan needs you. You have unique skills, and you bring something to this collage of life that nobody else does. So don't bury your nose in your phone and withhold your gifts from us.

You're better than you realize. It's funny—I often see people here underestimate their potential. Taiwan, and the people here, are capable of great things—but we lose sight of that in the "We're so small" mindset. Shake it off. It would be healthy to let go of the "We're so small" thinking. The next couple of years is going to be challenging for Taiwan—you need to be active, making and executing your plans; not isolating and killing time.

The Bill Gates quote at the start of this chapter comes from an interview he gave in 2013. His point is that human beings who are active in the world will solve problems. Starvation, poverty, infant deaths, malaria, clean drinking water—these things require human spirit, active involvement, connectedness, and engagement.

The world needs your head up.

加油!

Key Words

Ongoing (adj)—something that continues, never stops

Determine (v)—to evaluate, analyze, choose what value something has

9/11 (n)—September 11, 2001, terrorist attacks on the United States

Show a pattern (figure of speech)—things that are common or connected that indicate a trend

Deem (something) necessary (idiom)—to decide that something is important and needed

Content (adj)—satisfied with things

Big picture (n ph)—a view of the world that includes many people, things and time periods

Fantastic (adj)—super, great

Bring something to (something) (figure of speech)—to contribute something to a situation

Collage (n)—a combination of many images or ideas

Starvation (n)—not having enough food

Malaria (n)—a disease spread by mosquitos

Source for the Bill Gates quote:

About the author

Bill Quinn has lived in Taiwan since February, 2003, and for most of that time was with ORTV (Overseas Radio & Television). For nearly ten years, Bill hosted the Advanced Magazine daily radio program which is broadcasted daily in Taiwan and mainland China, and online at www.studioclassroom.com. He also appeared on the Studio Classroom 空中英語教室 and Let's Talk in English TV programs, the Advanced Magazine Topic Talks web video series, along with writing many articles for Advanced Magazine.

Bill also conducts corporate, university and government training programs in Taiwan, and has trained over 1,000 professionals and government servants in the areas of Effective Spoken and Written Business Communications, How to Give Effective English Presentations, How to Attend International Conferences Effectively, How to Conduct FDA (Food & Drug Administration) Inspections Overseas, APEC meeting procedures and a variety of industry-specific and government ministry-specific trainings.

A graduate of Pennsylvania State University, with a degree in Business Administration and Marketing, Bill spent nearly twenty years in America working in sales, marketing and manufacturing for companies such as Xerox, Barnett Bank, ADP (Automatic Data Processing) and Weyerhaeuser Paper.

Bill's first book, *The English Speech Contest*, helps students prepare, practice and deliver winning speeches (prepared and impromptu), while helping students develop confidence in public speaking. *The English Speech Contest* is also an instruction guide for teachers in helping them to assist their students in developing this lifelong skill.

In August, 2016, the Taiwan Government Ministry of Culture honored *The English Speech Contest* placing it on its list of recommended readings for junior and senior high school students.

You can find *The English Speech Contest* at www.books.com.tw,

or use this QR code for Jinni Publishing;